CULTURES OF THE WORLD
Paraguay

Cavendish
Square
New York

Published in 2019 by Cavendish Square Publishing, LLC
243 5th Avenue, Suite 136, New York, NY 10016

Library of Congress Cataloging-in-Publication Data

Names: Jermyn, Leslie, author. | Yong, Jui Lin, author. | Jones, Naomi E., author.
Title: Paraguay / Leslie Jermyn, Yong Jui Lin, and Naomi E. Jones.
Description: Third edition. | New York, NY : Cavendish Square Publishing, LLC, 2019. | Series: Cultures of the world | Includes bibliographical references and index.
Identifiers: LCCN 2018053810 (print) | LCCN 2018056022 (ebook) | ISBN 9781502647399 (ebook) | ISBN 9781502647382 (library bound)
Subjects: LCSH: Paraguay--History--Juvenile literature. | Paraguay--Civilization--Juvenile literature. | Paraguay--Social life and customs--Juvenile literature.
Classification: LCC F2668.5 (ebook) | LCC F2668.5 .J47 2020 (print) | DDC 989.2--dc23
LC record available at https://lccn.loc.gov/2018053810

Editorial Director: David McNamara
Editor: Kristen Susienka
Copy Editor: Nathan Heidelberger
Associate Art Director: Alan Sliwinski
Designer: Jessica Nevins
Production Coordinator: Karol Szymczuk
Photo Research: J8 Media

CONTENTS

PARAGUAY TODAY

PARAGUAY IS A SMALL, LANDLOCKED COUNTRY IN THE HEART OF South America. It has long been isolated from the world due to its geographic position and social conditions. Southeast Paraguay has beautiful forests and running rivers, while the northwest has a forbidding terrain that keeps most humans away.

ENVIRONMENTAL ISSUES

Paraguay has a subtropical climate and is home to a vast array of flora and fauna. Sadly, in the twenty-first century, the country faces several environmental crises. One of the most pressing is the rapid disappearance of forests. The ever-expanding production of soybeans has threatened both the eastern forest and the Chaco. The Chaco is a plain that stretches over the west of Paraguay and into Argentina and Bolivia. Also in the Chaco, cattle ranches have been a cause of deforestation. Rapid depletion of forests there has caused many plant and animal species to become endangered.

In addition, rural and indigenous, or native, people have lost a great deal of their land to beef and soy production.

THE PEOPLE

Paraguay has a population of nearly seven million people. Historically, Paraguay has been mainly rural, with about 55 to 70 percent of the population living in the countryside. This has changed in the twentieth and twenty-first centuries, however. Today, 61.6 percent of the population lives in urban areas. Major cities include the capital of Asunción, Ciudad del Este, and Encarnación.

Paraguayans are unique in that their modern culture is a blend of European and indigenous ones. Theirs is the only country in Latin America where the majority of the population speaks an indigenous language, Guaraní, rather than a European language. About 90 percent of Paraguayans speak Guaraní, especially in rural areas, and Spanish is primarily spoken in the cities. Guaraní heritage is very important to the history and culture of Paraguay, and can be observed in traditional food, music, and crafts.

A group of children pose for a photograph in Ciudad del Este.

Paraguay's economy has grown at an average of 4 percent annually since 2014, primarily due to export of hydroelectric power from the Itaipú Dam, soybeans, and livestock production. This economic growth has helped to reduce poverty, although income inequality is still very high. While Paraguay's poverty rate has declined in recent years due to a series of social reforms, it remains high, particularly in rural areas. About a quarter of the population is still below the poverty line. Inequality continues to rise in Paraguay, with new developments favoring the wealthy while ignoring the needs of the impoverished majority.

GOVERNMENT

For most of its history since it became an independent nation, Paraguay was governed by dictators. This often meant that the country was sealed off from the rest of the world or shunned by it. The first free elections were held in 1993 and were won by the conservative Colorado Party. Former bishop Fernando Lugo won a historic victory in Paraguay's presidential election on April 20, 2008, defeating the ruling party candidate and ending sixty-one years of conservative rule. Lugo won with nearly 41 percent of the vote, compared with almost 27 percent for Blanca Ovelar of the Colorado Party. However, Lugo was impeached four years later due to his failure to address issues relating to land rights. After Lugo's impeachment, the Colorado Party resumed the presidency with the 2013 election of Horacio Cartes, a successful businessman. His presidential term was marked by corruption scandals, increased deforestation of the Chaco, the abandonment of many of his predecessor's social policies, and little progress as far as his campaign promises went. Cartes was succeeded by Mario Abdo Benítez, another member of the Colorado Party, who was elected in April 2018. Abdo Benítez defeated Liberal Party candidate Efraín Alegre in one of the closest elections in Paraguayan history.

Paraguay may have faced difficult times in the past, but it has attempted to resurrect itself in the twenty-first century. It is working on positioning itself as a place where people should come and explore. It likewise is working to attract people to move there and call the country home.

GEOGRAPHY

The ceiba tree is one of the many varieties of plant life native to Paraguay.

1

THE REPUBLIC OF PARAGUAY IS situated in the heart of South America. Looking at a map of the country, the Paraguay River clearly divides it into two different parts, the Eastern region and the Western region. However, it can also be divided into four regions with varying landscapes and climates. East of the Paraguay River, rain forests and wetlands can be found. West of the river, the harsh Chaco plains begin. To the south of the Tropic of Capricorn, the climate is cooler and subtropical, while to the north, the climate is more tropical.

MAJOR FEATURES

Paraguay is one of only two South American countries that does not border an ocean (the other is Bolivia). Instead, it shares borders with Brazil in the east and northeast, Bolivia in the northwest, and Argentina from the southeast to the southwest. It has a surface area of 157,048 square miles (406,752 square kilometers), which makes it slightly smaller than the state of California. The capital city is Asunción. The Tropic of Capricorn

Paraguay has great natural beauty. Its outdoor attractions include waterfalls, mountains, and visiting a hydroelectric dam. Likewise, the Chaco is unique in its own way. About 2 percent of the population lives there, as its arid landscape offers little nourishment.

BOLIVIA

BRAZIL

Gran

Chaco

PARAGUAY

ARGENTINA

BRAZIL

Mayor Pablo Lagerenza

Bahía Negra

Fuerte Olimpo

Mariscal José Félix Estigarribia

Dr. Pedro P. Peña

Puerto La Victoria

Filadelfia

Bella Vista Norte

Pedro Juan Caballero

R. Apa

Yby Yaú

Horqueta

Capitán Bado

Fortín General Díaz

R. Monte Lindo

Pozo Colorado

Concepción

R. Verde

Fortín Rojas Silva

R. Pilcomayo

R. Aguaray Guazú

Salto del Guairá

R. Confuso

R. Aguaray Guazú

San Pedro del Ykuamandyju

Curuguaty

Lago Itaipú

Villa del Rosario

San Estanislao

Lago del Río Yguazú

Villa Hayes

Areguá

Coronel Oviedo

ASUNCIÓN

Caacupé

Itaipú

Ciudad del Este

Paraguarí

Cerro Peró 842 m

Santa Rita

Villarrica

Caazapá

María Auxiliadora

San Juan Bautista

Pilar

San Ignacio

Obligado

Paso de Patria

Ayolas

Coronel Bogado

Encarnación

Río Paraná

This map of Paraguay includes the country's main roads.

crosses the country at the town of Concepción.

There are three major rivers in Paraguay. The Paraná rises in Brazil and flows southward, defining the southeast and southern borders of Paraguay. The Paraguay, which gave the country its name, also has its source in Brazil and flows south through Paraguay. The Pilcomayo starts in the Andes Mountains and travels southeast, forming the border with Argentina. At Asunción, it joins the Paraguay, turns south, and continues to flow along the southwest border with Argentina.

The population is estimated to be seven million, but the people are not spread out evenly across the country. Approximately 98 percent of Paraguayans live east of the Paraguay River, although this region only makes up 40 percent of the land area. The largest area of land lies in the Chaco, but only 2 percent of the population lives there.

WEST OF THE RIVER

The Chaco Boreal (or simply the Chaco) is a broad plain with muddy and sandy soils. The Chaco is part of a larger area called Gran Chaco, which includes parts of northern Argentina and southern Bolivia. It has evolved over thousands of years from the dumping of silt by the rivers flowing down from the Andes Mountains in the west. Although the Chaco is almost uniformly flat, differences in rainfall produce areas of distinct vegetation: Low, Middle, and High Chaco.

In the Low Chaco, near the Paraguay River, the plains are underwater most of the year due to flooding from the river, and the soil does not absorb or drain water well. The landscape is dotted with marshes and ponds, caranday palm trees, and *monte* (MOHN-tay), a thorny scrub. Moving northwest, conditions become drier,

The ruins of the Jesuit *reducción* of Trinidad are on the Paraná Plateau.

with less groundwater and rainfall. Much of this area is scrub with groves of trees that have incredibly hard wood, a result of growing slowly. Some people manage to live in the Low and Middle Chaco despite the harsh conditions, but cultivation is difficult, so most rely on cattle ranching. The High Chaco, near the Bolivian border, is a dense scrub forest. Rainfall is unpredictable, and few people live here.

EAST OF THE RIVER

In contrast to the Chaco, travelers have characterized the Eastern, or Oriental, region as "paradise on Earth." There are plains, broad valleys, and forested plateaus. The highest peak, Cerro Pero, is 2,762 feet (842 meters) above sea level and lies in the San Rafael Cordillera in the southeast. Rainfall is more abundant and predictable in this region, making farming and forestry more productive. As well as being surrounded on the east, south, and west by large rivers, numerous smaller tributaries crisscross this region.

In eastern Paraguay, there are subregions characterized by differences in topography and vegetation. The most easterly portion is the Paraná Plateau, a forested area separated from the rest of eastern Paraguay by an escarpment. Around Asunción is the Central Hill Belt. This area is characterized by rolling hills with small isolated peaks and lakes. Its highest point is the city of Villarrica at 820 feet (250 m).

The word *chaco* comes from a Quechua word meaning "abundance of wildlife." (The Quechua are an indigenous group living in the Andes of Bolivia and Peru.)

Between the plateau in the east and the Central Hill Belt in the west is the Central Lowland. Here river valleys are broad and shallow and floods are common. Most of the lowland is a plain that gently rises to the plateau, but the landscape is dotted with thickly forested, flat-topped hills rising 20 to 30 feet (6 to 9 m) above the surrounding plain. These outcroppings cover anywhere from a few acres to a few miles and are known as *islas de monte*, or wooded islands.

Finally, in southwest Paraguay is the Ñeembucú Plain. The Tebicuary River, a major tributary of the Paraguay River, bisects this flat region. Most of this area is swampy, but there are swells of higher land that remain dry and permit people to live there. The eastern region is more amenable to human habitation because of its greater abundance of water and forest resources.

WEATHER AND SEASONS

Paraguay's climate is subtropical. The main determinants of the weather are the winds. In the summer months, October through March, warm, dust-laden winds blow in from the Amazon Basin in the north. In the winter, May through August, cold winds from the Andes blow across the Argentine plain into Paraguay. With no natural wind barriers such as mountain ranges along the way, the winds can reach speeds of 100 miles per hour (161 kilometers per hour) in southern Paraguay. Winds can also cause dramatic temperature changes in short periods of time.

There is no real spring or autumn in Paraguay, but April and September are transitional months between the two main seasons. Temperatures during these months are lower than the summer highs and may drop below freezing on occasion. Around Asunción, winter temperatures average 65 degrees Fahrenheit (18 degrees Celsius), while summer sees average temperatures of 75°F (24°C). In January, the hottest summer month, the daily average temperature is 84°F (29°C), and highs of 100°F (38°C) are common. It is much warmer in the Chaco, with highs over 100°F (38°C) being quite normal in the summer.

Rainfall is evenly distributed all year except for August, the driest month, and March to May and October to November, which are wetter than average. It rarely snows in Paraguay. Rainfall varies dramatically across the country.

In the far eastern forest belt, average rainfall is 67 inches (170 centimeters) per year; in the far western Chaco, it averages 20 inches (50 cm) per year. The problem with rainfall in the Chaco is not just the small quantity but the irregularity and the fact that rain evaporates very quickly in this arid environment. This contributes to the challenges of living in the region and limits the range of crops that can be grown. The average rainfall diminishes from east to west, with Asunción getting about 51 inches (130 cm) per year. However, due to global warming, conditions are changing. In 2007, Paraguay experienced a crippling drought that led to the worst forest fires in the nation's recorded history. Events like this may be more frequent in the future, as weather patterns shift due to global warming.

NATIVE PLANTS AND ANIMALS

The coatimundi is a relative of the raccoon.

Paraguay has generous amounts of useful and edible vegetation. There are around five hundred species of hardwood deciduous trees that can be used for lumber. The national tree, the *lepacho* (lay-PAH-choh), produces straight-grained hardwood and has multicolored flowers. The *quebracho* (kay-BRAH-choh) grows in the Chaco. Its wood is said to be stone-hard and is harvested for its tannin, a chemical used in leather processing. There are also eucalyptus, cedar, and ceiba trees. The most famous Paraguayan plant is the yerba maté (YAYR-bah MAH-tay), a relative of the holly family that grows wild in the eastern forests and is harvested to make maté tea. There are coconut palms, caranday palms, and palmitos, which produce the "palm hearts" we eat. There is a wild pineapple, *caraguatá* (kah-rah-gwah-TAH), that may be the predecessor of the modern plantation fruit. Orange trees grow wild, as does Indian corn. In the Chaco are grasses, cacti, and a bush resembling mesquite. However, deforestation in Paraguay has threatened forest populations in recent years. In 2013, a study reported that an area the size of the city of Manhattan was being culled every two weeks.

Although the Chaco does not hold much interest for people to live there, it is a wildlife haven. Jaguars, pumas, and ocelots hunt here—and there is a

As part of the 2013 Paraguay Biodiversity Project, conservation efforts have been made to protect the habitat of 296 bird species, including the bare-throated bellbird, Paraguay's national bird.

Paraguay has an array of wildlife living within it. From big cats and other mammals to fish and reptiles, the animal kingdom is alive in this country.

The range of the puma, or mountain lion, is among the largest of the land animals, stretching from northern Canada to southern Argentina. Pumas can live in mountains, forests, and open grasslands. Their pale brown to gray coat camouflages them in a wide variety of settings. They can jump as high as 18 feet (5.5 m) and kill their prey by breaking the spinal cord.

Paraguay's other big cat is the jaguar. Jaguars have spotted coats like their African cousin, the leopard. They live near water since their favorite prey is river reptiles. They can kill caimans and swat fish out of the water with a paw. Unlike most cats, jaguars swim. The jaguar—yaguareté (yah-gwahr-ay-TAY) in Guaraní—is the king of beasts in this region of the world and figures in many myths and legends. Sadly, the jaguar population has been decreasing in the twenty-first century due to habitat loss caused by agricultural expansion.

The tapir is one of the oddest-looking animals. When Paraguay was first discovered by Spanish explorers, reports reached Europe about an animal with the trunk of an elephant, the hooves of a horse, and the size and coloring of a cow. It was not until

lot to hunt. Among the larger mammals are peccaries, deer, giant anteaters, armadillos, tapirs, coatimundis, and capybaras. Reptiles include the deadly coral snake and the anaconda, a constrictor. The semiaquatic anaconda hangs from trees and waits for its prey. It can reach 30 feet (9 m) in length. Bird species are numerous, with over seven hundred species recorded. There are large ostrich-like rheas that stand about 5 feet (1.5 m) tall and tiny hummingbirds that fit in the palm of a child's hand. In between, there are ducks, pheasants, quail, partridges, kingfishers, egrets, herons, and storks. All of these species, however, face endangerment from deforestation that persists in the region.

1750 that the first accurate description was made. The tapir stands 4.5 feet (1.4 m) high and is up to 8 feet (2.5 m) long. The larger females can weigh up to 730 pounds (330 kg). Tapirs like to live near water and bathe daily. They also take mud baths to protect themselves from stinging insects. Tapirs live alone or in pairs and are favorite prey of pumas and jaguars. They are also being hunted for their hides and their meat. Around the world, these creatures' numbers are decreasing. It may become an endangered species if hunting continues.

Another odd animal found in Paraguay is the giant anteater. It can grow up to 7 feet (2 m) long and weigh 100 pounds (45 kg—a lot considering that it eats only ants and termites.) Anteaters catch their dinner with long tongues coated with sticky saliva. Since they have no teeth, the insects are ground up in the stomach by strong muscles. It takes about thirty thousand insects per day to feed one of these animals!

The piranha, the fish of movies and nightmares, lives in the Paraguay and Paraná Rivers and their tributaries. There are twenty species of piranha, but only four are carnivorous. All of them, however, have a mouth full of razor-sharp teeth. Their name derives from the Guaraní pirá rahi *(pee-RAH RAH-ee), meaning "tooth fish." After years of intensive study of the meat-eating species, scientists have concluded that piranha attacks are unpredictable. One thing scientists do know is that piranhas are attracted by fresh blood, and once they go into a feeding frenzy, they can reduce a cow to a skeleton in thirty minutes. They can measure up to 16 inches (40 cm) long. They are the favorite prey of caimans. As illegal trade reduces the population of caimans, piranhas are increasing in number.*

At least three hundred fish species have been cataloged in Paraguay's rivers. Sport fishermen covet the dorado, which can weigh up to 40 pounds (18 kilograms). There are also catfish, *mandi, manguruy,* and *pacú* (pah-KOO). Two of the stranger fish are piranhas and lungfish. The piranha is known for its sharp, flesh-eating teeth. The lungfish can survive low water levels by sealing itself in mud. The most eaten fish in Paraguay, the *surubí* (soo-roo-BEE), lives in the Paraguay and Paraná Rivers, feeding on bottom-dwelling fish. It can grow up to 5 feet (1.5 m) long and weigh up to 110 pounds (50 kg). Two species of caiman (a type of alligator) are also found in these rivers.

Eastern Paraguay has many of the same animals as the Chaco, but due to the expansion of human habitation and overhunting, they are restricted in numbers and usually found in the forests of the Paraná Plateau. There are a few animals not found in the Chaco, particularly birds of the parrot and parakeet families. The *Amazona aestiva*, or turquoise-fronted parrot, is called *loro hablador* (LOR-oh hah-blah-DOR) in Paraguay. That means "talkative parrot." It is green with red and blue wing feathers and has a blue and yellow head. It is about 14 inches (35 cm) long and has feet adapted to living on tree branches. Like other parrots, it can learn words and phrases when domesticated, and can even imitate people's voices. In the wild, it mates for life.

MAJOR CITIES

Paraguay's population has seen an explosion in recent decades, nearly tripling in size since 1970. By far the biggest gains have been in urban areas, with internal migration motivated first by the economic boom of the 1970s and later by economic recession in the countryside. In the twenty-first century, the country's population growth has slowed, but despite a trend of young Paraguayans emigrating to seek new opportunities outside the country, the nation's population continues to rise.

ASUNCIÓN   The full name of Paraguay's capital city is Nuestra Señora Santa María de la Asunción (Saint Mary, Our Lady of the Assumption), but most people know it only as Asunción. It has always been the administrative and economic center of Paraguay because of its location at the meeting of the Paraguay and Pilcomayo Rivers. The city is located strategically where the Paraguay River and surrounding hills form a natural fortress, a feature that was quite attractive to the first Spaniards who arrived in the early 1500s. Until the twentieth century, the only way to ship goods into or out of Paraguay was by the Paraguay River to the Atlantic Ocean via Buenos Aires in Argentina. This made Asunción the only real city in Paraguay for most of its history. Today the population of Asunción is approximately 525,000, and roughly 40 percent of Paraguay's 7 million people live within the Greater Asunción area.

CIUDAD DEL ESTE Although Asunción is by far the biggest city, Ciudad del Este grew enormously from a small town in 1957 to the second-largest city in Paraguay, with 293,000 people as of 2016. A major commercial center, Ciudad del Este generates about 60 percent of Paraguay's gross domestic product (GDP). There are two major attractions in Ciudad del Este: the hydroelectric project just outside the city at Itaipú and the Friendship Bridge across the Paraná River to Foz do Iguaçu in Brazil. Itaipú was started in 1975 and completed in 1982. The city is also the seat of the Roman Catholic diocese of Ciudad del Este. As the city grew, the lure of jobs attracted many poor rural dwellers.

Here is a view of the skyline of Asunción, the capital of Paraguay.

Asunción was founded in 1537, which makes it the oldest Spanish capital in southern South America. It was founded by accident. The third Spanish expedition to Río de la Plata, led by Pedro de Mendoza, attempted to settle at Buenos Aires in 1536, but an attack by indigenous people forced the settlers to flee up the Paraná River to Santa Fé. From there, one of the settlers was sent upriver to explore. When he failed to return, another expedition went upriver to look for him. On their way back, one of the crew, Juan de Salazar y Espinoza, stopped at the site of modern Asunción and founded a settlement. This happened on August 15, 1537, which on the Catholic calendar is the Feast of the Assumption—Asunción in Spanish.

From 1537 to 1617, Asunción was the center of Spanish activity for all of southern South America. Adventurers and settlers from Spain came here first before moving on. In this way, Asunción was the starting point for at least eight other important Spanish cities, including Buenos Aires, and was known as the "mother of cities." In 1617, Buenos Aires was separated from the province of Paraguay, and Asunción declined in importance to become a backwater of South American cities.

Today, the city has much to offer in terms of history, architecture, and government. The city is the home of the national government, the principal port, and the chief industrial and cultural center of the country. Local manufacturing production includes footwear, textiles, and tobacco products. Paraguay's only stock exchange, the BVPASA (Bolsa de Valores y Productos de Asunción), is located here. The city is home to the Museo Nacional de Bellas Artes, the Church of the Incarnation (Iglesia de Dios Encarnación), the Metropolitan Cathedral of Our Lady of the Assumption, and the National Pantheon of the Heroes, where many of the nation's heroes are entombed.

In addition, the road connection with Brazil has fostered a booming business in contraband goods, such as illegal weapons, counterfeit goods, and illicit substances, flowing in both directions. Another hydroelectric project at Yacyretá, outside Encarnación, and a bridge connecting this city with Argentina have fueled growth there too.

ROADS

There are numerous smaller towns scattered across the eastern region, but since less than 25 percent of Paraguay's roads are paved (mainly those that connect Asunción with Encarnación and Ciudad del Este), these towns retain a rural character.

The east and west offer striking contrasts—abundant water in the east, little or no water in the west; luxuriant eastern forests, dry grasses and leafless trees in the west; hills and meadows in the east, and flat prairie in the west; lots of people in the east, almost no one in the west. They could almost be separate countries, but Paraguayans consider both sides of the Paraguay River to be complementary and equally important to their identity.

Between 2008 and 2016, the World Bank financed the Paraguay Road Maintenance Project, which was intended to drastically improve Paraguay's roads. The project led to increased road access for multiple towns in central and southern Paraguay.

INTERNET LINKS

http://www.faunaparaguay.com
Here you can find an information archive on Paraguayan animals and natural history.

https://www.lonelyplanet.com/Paraguay
This website contains news and other information about the country.

https://www.nytimes.com/interactive/2017/11/23/travel/what-to-do-36-hours-in-asuncion-paraguay.html
This article explores one person's visit to Paraguay's capital city, Asunción, in 2017.

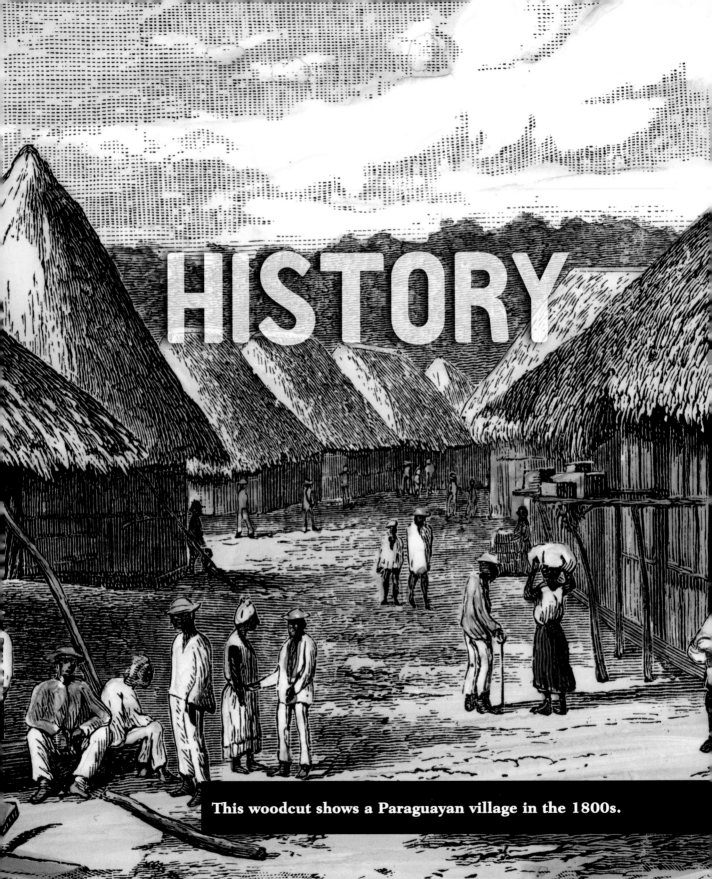

HISTORY

This woodcut shows a Paraguayan village in the 1800s.

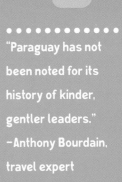

2

PARAGUAY WAS THE FIRST SOUTH American country to become independent. This may seem surprising considering Paraguay's turbulent history. Immediately following independence in 1811, there was a series of dictators and several disastrous wars. However, Paraguayans persevered and overcame these circumstances.

THE GUARANÍ

The first people to settle in Paraguay were not Europeans but an indigenous tribe called the Guaraní. They occupied the eastern forest region. However, when the Europeans arrived in the 1500s, this group may have consisted of many subgroups that were known by different names. The Guaraní lived in small villages of one hundred to three hundred people. They combined farming in the forest with hunting, fishing, and gathering wild fruits and vegetables. Their main staples were corn and manioc, a root used to make flour. They also grew sweet potatoes, peanuts, pumpkins, bananas, papayas, and watermelons. To supplement this diet, they gathered wild foods, such as honey and palm nuts, and hunted tapirs and deer. They also fished using wooden hooks or baskets.

A village would usually have four to eight large communal houses up to 165 feet (50 m) long. Everyone living in a house together was related

Here is an artistic representaion of life on the Paraguay River in the 1800s.

through their male relatives. The men of a village would elect an informal chief, but much of the real power rested with the shamans, or religious practitioners. Villages were seminomadic, meaning that when the fertility of the soil was exhausted after many years of planting, the whole village would move to a new area of the forest to farm fresh land.

LIVING IN THE CHACO

In the Chaco, there were at least five different language groups. In this hostile environment, the indigenous people survived by combining a little farming with much hunting and the gathering of wild foods. They hunted deer, peccaries, tapirs, and rheas, and in areas with rivers, they fished with nets. Women generally did the gathering of food, things such as edible cacti and waterlily roots. On their small farms, they grew corn, yucca, and beans. Chaco groups lived in smaller villages and were also seminomadic to exploit resources in different areas. Their leaders were people who were very good at mediating conflicts and at persuading people to do things. These chiefs could not order people around; they could only ask or persuade gently.

Before the Spaniards arrived, there had been conflict among some of these groups. The Guaraní, in particular, had been expanding over the previous two thousand years so that by the 1500s, they occupied a huge area covering much of the Amazon Basin and parts of Uruguay, Paraguay, and Argentina. This expansion was not always peaceful. Guaraní fought with local groups in order to take over their land. The Chaco groups closest to the Paraguay River periodically had to defend themselves against Guaraní invasions from across the river. This was the situation when the Europeans arrived.

EUROPEAN CONQUEST

The first European to see the land that would become Paraguay was Alejo García, a Portuguese explorer. García was shipwrecked off the coast of Brazil and learned to live with the Guaraní of that area. From them he learned of a mythical "white king" in the interior who had mountains of gold and silver. In 1524, he set off with a few Guaraní to explore the interior of the continent. He passed through eastern Paraguay, where the local Guaraní volunteered two thousand men to accompany him to fight the white king. This group crossed the Chaco and reached the edges of the Inca Empire in Peru. There they managed to steal quite a lot of gold and silver before the Inca chief chased them out. On his way back to the coast, García and his party were murdered by another group of indigenous people. For the next thirty years, similar stories about precious metals would entice Europeans to come to Paraguay.

Another important figure in Paraguay's history is Domingo Martinez de Irala, a Spanish explorer. He became Asunción's governor, established its laws, and made it a main base. He also encouraged association between Spanish explorers and the native people. However, he also established a system of servitude among the Guaraní. Before long, Paraguay would be at the center of Spanish power in South America.

Asunción was settled in 1537 because it was a good site for a fort and the local Guaraní people were quite friendly. They welcomed the Spaniards with food and hospitality because they hoped these strange warriors would help them beat their enemies in the Chaco. Of course, the Spaniards were not interested in fighting indigenous people who had no gold or silver, nor did they particularly want to settle at Asunción; they just wanted a camp from which to travel farther westward, where they hoped to find the rumored city of gold and silver. By the 1550s, enthusiasm for exploration was waning. The Spaniards had discovered that if they managed to cross the Chaco and the Andes, they simply found themselves in the new Spanish colony of Peru. They decided to settle the land as best they could.

The new settlers introduced *encomienda* (ehn-coh-mee-EHN-dah), a system designed to give each European rights to the labor and tribute of a number of Guaraní, in return for his protection. In places such as Mexico and Peru with large populations of indigenous people organized in complex farming societies, this system made some Spaniards very rich. In Paraguay, where the native people had been hunters and gatherers and their populations were spread out, there was little wealth to be taken or earned. Part of the problem was Paraguay's isolation from other colonies.

SPANISH-GUARANÍ HERITAGE

Two conditions in Paraguay changed the face of the nation permanently: the nature of the social structure of the native population and isolation from Spain. The Guaraní had developed tribes and governmental systems, but the Spanish did not understand this when they arrived.

When the Spaniards attempted to "govern" them, they found it very difficult to organize the Guaraní. If Asunción had been better connected with the other colonial settlements in South America, the Spaniards might have persevered in trying to change the Guaraní way of life. But being far from their countrymen and having no wealth to trade or travel, they decided instead to adapt to the life of the Guaraní. Each Spaniard was assigned a group of Guaraní under the encomienda *system and chose to live among them. The Spaniards also took Guaraní wives; each settler had up to twenty wives. This meant, in turn, that lots of mestizo children were born.*

After only one generation, the rulers of the encomiendas *were these children. By the 1700s, they outnumbered the Guaraní. Interestingly, the children of Spanish-Guaraní relations grew up speaking Guaraní, not Spanish, since their mothers and the majority of the population spoke Guaraní. This is the basis for the modern population of Paraguay.*

In the 1600s, descendants of the settlers realized they could grow two crops near Asunción: yerba maté and tobacco. Both crops were traded with Spain for goods not available locally. By this time, the children of the first Spanish-Guaraní unions controlled the land and its wealth, such as it was. During the 1700s, they began to resent Spanish colonial power over trade and government. More Spaniards had arrived in Asunción in the 1700s, once they realized there was some money to be made in farming. There was friction between the two groups: the rural, Guaraní-speaking mestizo (mixed) elite and the Spanish-born and Spanish-speaking urban and government elite. In 1776, the affairs of Paraguay were put formally under the control of Buenos Aires, which was also controlled by Spain and was 1,000 miles (1,609 km) away. At the same time, the Spanish king increased taxes on Paraguayan exports, and this threatened to make trade impossible for Paraguayans. It was the beginning of the end for Spain's control over its most isolated colony.

FREEDOM FROM SPAIN

The story of how Paraguay became the very first independent nation in all of South America is quite confusing. It all started in Europe when the French ruler Napoleon took over the Spanish crown in 1808. Settlers in the New World, as the Americas were called, who were loyal to Spain did not accept French rule. Consequently, in 1810, the local government of Buenos Aires expelled the French representative of the crown, claiming that it would protect Spain's interests until a legitimate Spanish king sat on the throne again.

The leaders in Buenos Aires decided they would try to bring many other colonies under their control, by force if necessary. The mestizos of Paraguay had no intention of taking orders from Buenos Aires, however, once Buenos Aires no longer represented the Spanish king. An army from Buenos Aires arrived from down river in 1810, and mestizos and Spaniards fought together to resist it.

The Spaniards left the battlefield the minute things looked bad. Despite this, the mestizos managed to repel the army from Buenos Aires. When the Spanish governor returned to assume command of the mestizos, he found that they despised and ridiculed him as a coward. He tried to disband and disarm them, but could no longer command their obedience.

In 1811, a Portuguese army lieutenant visited the governor in Asunción. The mestizos thought he was there to offer Portuguese Brazil's support to the Spaniards. (He was not, but rumors can be very powerful.) Having long considered the Portuguese their enemy, the mestizos perceived this visit as an act of treason. On May 17, 1811, they declared Paraguay independent of Spain.

DICTATORSHIPS

For a few years following this declaration of independence, Paraguayans were quite paranoid that forces from either Buenos Aires or Brazil would try to take over their new country. From among the first five men appointed to rule the country, one man stood out as Paraguay's hope in avoiding invasion—José Gaspar Rodríguez de Francia. A lawyer, he negotiated an agreement with

The mestizos and the Spaniards of Paraguay joined forces to fight the army from Buenos Aires in 1810, but they fought for different reasons. The Spaniards believed (incorrectly) that Buenos Aires was fighting to free the colonies from all control by Europe. The mestizos, on the other hand, had in the past resented control from Spain through Buenos Aires. They had welcomed their freedom from this control when France took over the Spanish crown; they had no intention of going back to the status quo.

the leaders in Buenos Aires to leave Paraguay alone. Most Paraguayans were uneducated mestizo farmers; they were overly impressed with Francia's skills and knowledge. He convinced them, along with the urban elite, that he was indispensable. Anyone who was not convinced was killed or jailed by Francia's supporters. He was elected to the post of supreme dictator of Paraguay in 1814, and in 1816 a meeting of citizens declared him dictator for life.

Francia's tenure was a mixed blessing for Paraguay. He closed the borders in 1818, forbidding anyone to enter or leave. He overtaxed the urban elite and confiscated the land of the rural elite. The average farmer gained by these measures, as land was leased to them very cheaply and surplus state-owned livestock was given away for free. On the negative side, Francia spent almost no money on education or public works, and he did not allow free speech or democracy in any form. He knew his enemies were likely to be other educated Europeans, so he terrorized them with torture and repression. He even made it illegal for European-born people to marry one another. They had to marry people of mixed ethnicity or indigenous people. This was to ensure that they mixed with groups that were more supportive of him and did not form a tight-knit group among themselves. Francia died in 1840. Although he was often cruel and despotic, he had been honest. He never drew his salary nor did he tamper with the property and riches he took for the state.

In the year after Francia's death, there was chaos in Paraguay. Finally, in 1841, another dictator for life was named—Francia's nephew, Carlos Antonio López. He released Francia's six hundred political prisoners but still forbade free speech. López was not as honest as his uncle had been with public money, but he did spend some of it to build rural roads and four hundred elementary schools. He also financed many new industries in Asunción, including textile production, arms manufacture, and a railroad, one of the first in South America. Paraguay was almost progressive under López. When he died in 1862, a congress of citizens elected his son Francisco Solano López as the new ruler.

The second López was less gifted than his father in foreign affairs. A policy of neutrality had been Paraguay's protection from invasion by larger powers. Francisco Solano López built up the army and tried to get Uruguay to form an alliance with him against Brazil and Argentina. These two nations had much bigger armies, and Uruguay declined to fight them. In 1864, Francisco Solano López declared war on Brazil, and the War of the Triple Alliance began.

Francisco Solano López was Paraguay's third dictator.

PARAGUAY AT WAR

When the war started, it was between Paraguay and Brazil. Francisco Solano López sought permission to move troops through Argentine territory. When his request was denied, he did so anyway, and this led Argentina to join the war. Uruguay was forced to join the alliance of Argentina and Brazil.

Paraguayan soldiers fought bravely for six years, but their beleaguered forces had little chance of victory. After three years of fighting, sixty thousand Paraguayan soldiers were dead. Another sixty thousand were drafted, including children under the age of fourteen, slaves, and old men. Meanwhile, women worked for the war effort behind the scenes. Many soldiers had no guns, and the cavalry was short on horses. The triple alliance occupied Asunción by 1869 and decimated the army there. Having fled north, Francisco Solano López carried on his own guerrilla war until he was killed at the battle of Cerro Corá in 1870. The war ended with López's death.

EFFECTS OF THE WAR

This war did not claim anywhere near the millions killed in the two World Wars of the twentieth century, but the impact on Paraguay in the nineteenth century was horrendous. The war's effects were felt in three areas: population, economy, and territory.

The Battle of Curupayty was fought on September 22, 1866. It was part of the War of the Triple Alliance.

When the war began, Paraguay had 525,000 people with a roughly equal proportion of men and women. Six years later, only 221,000 people were left. Of the survivors, 106,000 were adult women, another 86,000 were children, and only 28,000 were adult men. It would take Paraguay generations to recover a normal population distribution.

The second major effect of the war was economic. The victors imposed a huge fine on Paraguay to help pay for the costs of the war. This is standard practice when a country loses a war that it started, but this debt was too big for a poor country with few able-bodied workers. Eventually, the government had to sell many of the country's assets to pay its debts, and this affected the future of all Paraguayans into the twentieth century.

The third result of the war was that Paraguay was forced to give up territory to the two main victorious nations, Brazil and Argentina. Argentina took productive land in the southeast, while Brazil took land in the northeast. Paraguay lost Iguazú Falls, one of the world's natural wonders, to Argentina too. In total, 55,000 square miles (142,450 sq km) of territory were lost.

A NEW SYSTEM

The victorious forces occupied Asunción and controlled the government for six years. One of their first acts was to create the first constitution in Paraguay's history. Based on the United States and Argentine constitutions, it called for democracy and a separation of powers. For a country that had only seen government by dictators, this was too foreign a model. The 1870 constitution meant little in Paraguay.

With the new political system, two groups emerged: the Blues, or Grand Club, and the Reds, or Club of the People. They later became the Liberal Party and the Colorado Party, respectively. The Colorados were former supporters of López, while the majority of the Liberals had collaborated with the alliance. There were several former López supporters among the Liberals as well. These parties were not based on ideas but on personal loyalties. Each group struggled to get its members into power in order to control state resources. The Colorados held power until 1904, when the Liberals started a rebellion. The Liberals' victory initiated thirty-two years of Liberal governments. This period of Paraguayan history was totally chaotic. There were twenty-two separate administrations (only one of them was Colorado), and a fourteen-month civil war broke out in 1922. The Colorados had ruled with military strongmen during the nineteenth and early twentieth centuries, and the Liberals continued this trend, only exchanging military generals for rich businessmen. At no time was there anything like democracy, and the common people were virtually ignored by the government.

The Liberals might have held power indefinitely, but they made serious errors in dealing with neighboring Bolivia. Bolivia expanded its control of the Chaco in the late 1920s when it found oil in its part of the Chaco and suspected that the Paraguayan Chaco also contained reserves. Bolivia believed that Paraguay's army was too disorganized and underfunded to defend the territory. By 1932, border hostilities made war inevitable.

During the three-year Chaco War (1932—1935), the Paraguayan army fought hard to push the Bolivians back, and the horrible Chaco climate helped. Most of the Bolivian army consisted of indigenous people who lived in Bolivia's cold mountain areas. They suffered in the heat and did not know how to find water in the Chaco's desert climes. Both sides, however, suffered terrible losses. In 1935, exhausted, they signed a peace treaty. Paraguay got most of the Chaco area (there was no oil in it, after all) and in return, it gave Bolivia access to the sea via the Paraguay River.

Many people were not happy with the way the Liberals had managed the war. They tried to appease the soldiers by giving them a pension, or retirement money, but it was too little, too late. On February 17, 1936, in what is called the February Revolution, the military took control. Although it held power for the next eighteen years, politics in Paraguay looked pretty much the same as always: chaotic. Political infighting as well as disagreements with groups

Alfredo Stroessner was president of Paraguay from 1954 to 1989.

outside the government prevented stability. From 1946 to 1947, the country was once again plunged into civil war. One army officer who distinguished himself in this skirmish was Alfredo Stroessner.

STROESSNER'S GOVERNMENT

By 1954, Stroessner was one of the few individuals in Paraguay to hold power effectively. When the president of the time tried to curb his influence, Stroessner forcibly took office. No one knew it then, but Paraguay had returned once more to a long-term dictatorship.

Like his predecessors in the nineteenth century, Stroessner held power by exiling or killing his opponents. Unlike his predecessors, he held elections, thus observing the requirements of constitutional amendments he instituted in 1967. This constitution called for a bicameral legislature with two-thirds of the seats held by the political party that won elections and the rest divided among the opposition. Stroessner campaigned like any other politician, but with his absolute control of the army and support from wealthy Paraguayans, he never lost a vote. The congress was always filled with his Colorado supporters, who approved whatever he decided.

Opposition to Stroessner's virtual dictatorship mounted in the 1970s, both internally and internationally. The Catholic Church and Amnesty International, an organization dedicated to protecting human rights, criticized his abuse of human rights, particularly the rights of indigenous people. Others argued against Stroessner's approach of having anyone thought to be "subversive" imprisoned and tortured until they confessed, although many had committed no crime at all. US President Jimmy Carter also criticized the regime, demanding changes. Stroessner gave in a little by releasing some political prisoners.

After a period of economic success in the late 1970s, Paraguay suffered a recession. By then, Stroessner had run out of resources to exchange for support and was forced to borrow money from abroad. By 1985, governing was becoming more difficult, and Stroessner's health was failing. Even so, he

General Andrés Rodríguez Pedotti began his military career in 1942. He enlisted and, four years later, graduated from the country's military school, and then went on to serve the military.

When Stroessner became president, Rodríguez had risen to the rank of captain. By 1970, he was second-in-command of the military and a close confidant of Stroessner's. No one expected what happened in 1989. On the night of February 3, Rodríguez toppled Stroessner from power, proclaiming himself acting president. He vowed to his fellow citizens to allow fair elections when the time came.

International critics thought Rodríguez was just pretending to change the system and had just taken over from Stroessner. After all, he had been Stroessner's second-in-command and had become very rich during his friend's years as president. However, he proved them wrong in 1993 by calling for elections and later stepping down to election winner Juan Carlos Wasmosy. Rodríguez took up a seat as a senator for life.

still ran for leadership of the Colorado Party in 1987 and won. In 1989, however, one of his supporters, General Andrés Rodríguez, decided that enough was enough. He tried to arrest Stroessner in his home; after a gunfight between Rodríguez's troops and Stroessner's personal guard, Stroessner surrendered. He was later exiled to Brazil, where he lived out the rest of his days, dying in 2006 at ninety-three years old.

MODERN PARAGUAY

General Rodríguez started the process of creating democratic institutions. On June 18, 1992, a new constitution was approved that prevented anyone from having absolute control of the country.

On May 9, 1993, Colorado candidate Juan Carlos Wasmosy was elected with 39 percent of the vote. While Wasmosy was in office, there were accusations of corruption and concern that the military would return to power. However, he maintained government control until elections were held in May 1998. The Colorado candidate, Raúl Alberto Cubas Grau, won.

Cubas Grau was not in office long. When his vice president was assassinated in March 1999, he resigned amid civil unrest in the capital city and went into exile in Brazil. Senate leader Luis González Macchi became president. His government suffered many allegations of corruption, and González Macchi himself was found not guilty in a Senate impeachment trial involving corruption and mismanagement charges in February 2003.

In April 2003, Colorado candidate Nicanor Duarte Frutos was elected president. Duarte worked constructively with an opposition-controlled Congress, removing from office six Supreme Court justices suspected of corruption and enacting major tax reforms. Economic performance improved significantly under the Duarte administration, with inflation falling significantly and the government clearing its arrears with international creditors.

Mario Abdo Benítez and his wife greet the crowd at his inauguration in 2018.

On April 20, 2008, former Roman Catholic bishop Fernando Lugo (representing a coalition of opposition parties) was elected. Popular with landless peasants, Lugo had identified the reduction of corruption and economic inequality as two of his priorities. However, the Colorado Party held a majority in the Senate and blocked most of his major proposals. He was impeached in 2012, following a land dispute between peasants and wealthy landowners during which seventeen people were killed.

In April 2013, millionaire businessman-turned-politician Horacio Cartes was elected president, putting the Colorado Party back in control. Cartes was one of the richest men in Paraguay. His supporters believed that since he was a responsible businessman, that would translate into him accomplishing a lot to improve the country. Cartes promised to improve Paraguay's waterway and highway infrastructure, and encouraged foreign companies to invest in Paraguay. He led the country until the next elections in 2018.

Mario Abdo Benítez, the son of Stroessner's private secretary, was elected president in April 2018 in one of the closest elections in Paraguayan history. During his campaign, he promised to work to attract foreign investors, improve the tax system, and improve Paraguay's infrastructure.

Modern Paraguayans have a lot to be proud of with regard to rebuilding their country after several devastating wars. The Paraguayan culture and national identity, a blend of native Guaraní and Spanish heritage, has been kept alive throughout many hardships.

INTERNET LINKS

http://colonialparaguay.blogspot.com
This blog contains research about colonial Paraguay.

http://warfarehistorynetwork.com/daily/military-history/ war-of-the-triple-alliance-bloodbath-in-paraguay
Explore a detailed history of the War of the Triple Alliance at this web page.

GOVERNMENT

Here is a view of a session of the Paraguayan

3

PARAGUAY HAS HISTORICALLY BEEN vulnerable to dictators, but the 1992 constitution was written to prevent another Alfredo Stroessner from taking control. With the return to democracy, the government and political parties can operate as they were intended to under the constitution. Today, Paraguay is a presidential representative democratic republic.

GOVERNMENT IN ACTION

The president of Paraguay is both the head of state and the head of government. The president is selected through multiparty elections, and each presidential term lasts five years. The government has been primarily dominated by the Colorado Party, with the exception of Fernando Lugo, who was president from 2008 to 2012 and a member of the Patriotic Alliance for Change.

Executive power is exercised by the government. Legislative (lawmaking) power is vested in both the government and the two chambers of the National Congress, the Chamber of Senators and the Chamber of Deputies.

Paraguay's constitution, passed on June 20, 1992, is a remodeled version of the one passed under Stroessner in 1967. Government power is centered in the executive branch—the office of the president, the vice president, and the cabinet. Like the president, the vice president is elected to a five-year term. Meanwhile, the twelve-member cabinet is appointed by the president. The president is limited to serving a single term in office. In 2017, a constitutional amendment was proposed that would extend the presidential term limit, but it ultimately was defeated in the Chamber of Senators.

Below the president is a bicameral congress, which has an eighty-member Chamber of Deputies and a forty-five-member Chamber of Senators. These representatives are elected at the same time as the president for the same duration. Citizens eighteen years old and above are eligible to vote. The country is divided into seventeen departments, or sections, plus the capital city, Asunción. Each of these areas is administered by a governor, who is also elected every five years.

All judges are appointed by a six-member Council of Magistrates, an independent body that also appoints the electoral tribunal that oversees elections. The council is made up of elected members from the president's office (including the cabinet), congress, and the bar association (lawyers' group). The council's choices must be approved by the Chamber of Senators and the president. The highest court in the country is the Supreme Court. It has nine justices, or judges. Justices of the peace deal with minor cases in smaller courts. The attorney general's office assigns officials to all judicial departments in the country.

The most important changes in the new constitution were ones that protect the people from dictatorial control: the president can only hold office for a single term, and both houses of the legislature are elected by direct vote. Previously, the party with the most votes automatically got two-thirds of the seats in Congress. Now it may win the presidency but not have a clear majority in the legislature. Finally, the new constitution calls for the justice system to be separated from presidential control. Today, an elected body, not the president, is in charge of suggesting members of the Supreme Court. This, too, serves to limit the power of any individual. Nevertheless, power is still concentrated in the center. Important decisions are made by the national government, not department governors.

COLORADOS AND LIBERALS

The most powerful political party since 1954 has been the Colorado Party (National Republican Association). This party was founded in 1880 and supports a strong state and military. It held power until 1904 and regained control of the government by supporting Stroessner's coup in 1954. Stroessner distributed favors through the party's huge network to guarantee its support during elections. After he was exiled, party affiliation no longer meant favors from the government, but many people remained loyal to the Colorados out of family tradition.

The Liberal Party was established in 1887 and formed a government in 1904 when it won a civil war against the Colorados. It supports laissez-faire economics, meaning that it opposes state control of the economy. This policy did not work well after the Great Depression, and this, combined with the Liberal failure to direct the Chaco War, led to its downfall in 1936. The Liberals took over again briefly from 1939 to 1940. The party has found it difficult to compete against the resources of the Colorados, and personal rivalries between its leaders have contributed to the weakness of the party.

A *caudillo* (cow-DEE-yoh) is a strongman—someone who controls people's loyalty through a combination of threats and rewards. Most of Paraguay's leaders since independence have been *caudillos*, including José Gaspar Rodríguez de Francia, Carlos Antonio López, and Alfredo Stroessner.

A child displays the Colorado Party flag at Mario Abdo Benítez's inauguration.

Paraguay's
constitution has
been amended
twice in recent
years, once in
2011 and again
in 2014.

In the 1990s, however, there was opposition from another source. A strong social movement arose in rural areas to protest against the growing land shortage for poor farmers. It demanded possession of large landholdings that the Stroessner regime had awarded illegally—under the guise of "land reform"—to army generals and political followers.

Today, agriculture is a backbone of Paraguayan society. More than 17 percent of the country's economy comes from agriculture. Its farmers make significant contributions to Paraguayans and international partners every day.

PRESIDENTS IN RECENT YEARS

Andrés Rodríguez's term as president opened doors for others to follow through democratic elections. In the decades since the 1992 constitution was implemented, however, presidencies have been far from perfect.

JUAN CARLOS WASMOSY   After Wasmosy was elected on May 9, 1993, his government did not run smoothly because his Colorado Party had not achieved a majority in either house of the legislature. Opposition parties formed coalitions, or joint forces, and together with some dissatisfied Colorados, they effectively blocked presidential initiatives. His attempts to get all factions to agree to govern together rather than block every initiative were stymied because there were so many controversial problems requiring immediate attention, which stirred up disagreement. Some people within the government itself were not happy with Wasmosy's leadership. In 1996, General Lino Oviedo engineered a military coup against him. Its plans were never actualized, and Oviedo tried to run for president in 1998. However, Wasmosy was still bitter, and had Oviedo sentenced to ten years in prison for his attempts at overthrowing him. Oviedo was freed by Wasmosy's successor, Raúl Alberto Cubas Grau, after serving only a few months of his sentence.

RAÚL ALBERTO CUBAS GRAU   Like Wasmosy before him, Cubas Grau was an engineer. In 1998, he contested for president and won that year's May election. Seven months later, however, he resigned following a controversy that arose when he freed General Lino Oviedo from a ten-year prison sentence. Oviedo's release led to civil unrest and the assassination of the Paraguayan vice president, Luis María Argaña, on March 23, 1999, the country's tenth anniversary of democracy. The US Embassy in Asunción helped in negotiations that led to a transfer of power from Cubas Grau to Luis González Macchi.

LUIS GONZÁLEZ MACCHI   The González Macchi government achieved a consensus among the parties on many controversial issues, including economic reform. In 2003, Nicanor Duarte Frutos was elected and sworn in as president.

NICANOR DUARTE   Óscar Nicanor Duarte Frutos grew up during the Stroessner administration and was affiliated with Stroessner's Colorado Party at the age of fourteen while attending high school. He took office on August 15, 2003, becoming the eleventh consecutive Colorado Party president. Price inflation fell dramatically between 2003 and 2004, from 14.2 percent to a thirty-year low of 4.3 percent. President Duarte's economic reforms and austerity programs produced results more rapidly than many expected. He was succeeded by Fernando Lugo, who took office on August 15, 2008.

FERNANDO LUGO   When Fernando Lugo, a former bishop, led a march and rally in March 2006 at Asunción, he was immediately catapulted to the national political arena. Lugo ran in the 2008 presidential elections as a consensus candidate for the fractured opposition. He won, ending the Colorados' uninterrupted sixty-one-year rule—the longest-serving party in continuous office anywhere in the world.

Fernando Lugo was committed to addressing the enormous inequality of income distribution and had a "pro-poor" reputation. He benefited from the fact that the Catholic Church had a high standing among the public as a relatively honest institution in a country where corruption was rife. However, in 2009 he faced scandal when a woman claimed that he had fathered her child while he was still a bishop. Lugo later admitted to this.

Lugo was impeached in 2012 after a land dispute between poor farmers and wealthy landowners that left seventeen people dead. He had promised

to redistribute land to the farmers but had not kept his promise, and this resulted in violence. The impeachment proceedings went through both houses of Congress in only two days. Lugo's vice president, Federico Franco, took over between Lugo's removal from office and the next election later that year. The Colorado Party regained the presidency in 2013 with the election of Horacio Cartes.

HORACIO CARTES Cartes, a wealthy businessman, campaigned on the claim that the people of Paraguay must put aside their political differences and start working together in order to reduce poverty, increase capital, and move their country ahead in the world economy. He also promised to improve the waterway and highway infrastructure and encouraged foreign companies to invest in Paraguay.

During his campaign, he was accused several times of illegal activity, including drug trafficking, money laundering, and smuggling. However, his suspicious reputation did not prevent him from being elected. Throughout his presidency, Cartes had difficulty keeping his promises of social and economic change, as the gap between rich and poor in Paraguay continued to increase.

Prior to the 2018 elections, Cartes attempted to change the constitution in order to run for reelection. His proposal led to a series of violent demonstrations and street protests in the capital. After the storming and burning of the congress building by protesters, Cartes dropped the proposal. Instead, Mario Abdo Benítez, another Colorado Party candidate, was elected in April 2018.

MARIO ABDO BENÍTEZ Abdo Benítez is the son of Stroessner's private secretary and was living in the United States at the end of Stroessner's regime. He served in the Paraguayan air force, and received his education in the United States. Abdo Benítez is part of a movement seeking change within the Colorado

Party. Like Cartes, he promised during his campaign to work to attract foreign investors and improve the country's infrastructure.

Paraguay's government has seen many highs and lows throughout the country's existence. Today, it is still finding its footing in some places, while progressing into the twenty-first century.

INTERNET LINKS

https://www.bbc.com/news/world-latin-america-45200965
This article explores the swearing-in as president of Abdo Benítez in 2018.

https://www.britannica.com/place/Paraguay/Government -and-society
Visit this website for information about Paraguay's government and society.

https://www.theguardian.com/world/2017/apr/01/paraguays -congress-set-on-fire-after-vote-to-let-president-run-again
This article examines the people's protests in 2017 against Cartes's bid for a constitutional change that would allow him to run for reelection.

ECONOMY

Soybean farms like this one are common in Paraguay.

4

I N 2010, PARAGUAY HAD THE THIRD-fastest-growing economy in the world. It is dominated by agriculture, as it has always been. The economy has stayed relatively healthy for the last decade, and the cost of living has risen a great deal. However, hardships and poverty remain.

In the 2010s, the government has taken steps to diversify the economy. The number of factories operating in Paraguay has tripled since 2014. Historically, long-term growth and foreign investment have been limited by corruption and poor infrastructure, although Paraguay has worked hard in the twenty-first century to attract foreign investment by improving its infrastructure.

AN ECONOMY OF AGRICULTURE

For most of its early history, Paraguay exported a few agricultural products such as tobacco, yerba maté, and animal hides to Argentina. Under the dictatorship of José Gaspar Rodríguez de Francia (1814–1840), the state controlled most of the land, which was leased out to small farmers, and prohibited foreigners from living in Paraguay. Carlos Antonio López (1844–1862) allowed foreigners to enter the country and invest in business, but there was little to attract foreign businesspeople.

After the disastrous War of the Triple Alliance, economics in Paraguay changed. Successive governments had to cope with a huge war debt to Argentina and Brazil, which they tried to repay by selling Paraguay to foreign interests. This trend continued into the twentieth century so that by 1935, a mere nineteen companies owned half the economic wealth of the country.

By the time Stroessner came to power in 1954, he had to enforce stiff measures to control inflation and stabilize the currency. He depended on loans from countries such as the United States to support his programs. Internally, because he had absolute control, he could force businesspeople to accept his changes. He also took direct control of certain areas of the economy, such as railroads, shipping, meat processing, alcohol production, and telecommunications. He made it very attractive for foreign companies to do business in Paraguay. There were almost no taxes to be paid, and the regime was stable under Stroessner's iron hand. Throughout this period, the economy remained primarily agricultural, though this was slowly changing. In short, during Stroessner's early years, the economy grew very slowly, was primarily agricultural, and was dependent on large loans from foreign countries to make ends meet.

All this was to change in the mid-1970s when construction of the Itaipú Hydroelectric Dam started on the Paraná River in cooperation with Brazil. The project created jobs, and whole new sectors of the economy developed in construction and services for the workers. The promise of lucrative government contracts and cash wages piqued the interest of rich and poor alike. Many relocated to Itaipú, where a new city developed almost overnight at Ciudad del Este. At the same time, the government sponsored a land settlement program to promote farming in the eastern border regions. It offered parcels of state land at a low cost at a time when export crops like soybeans and cotton were in demand on the international market. Increased contact between Brazil and Paraguay over the Friendship Bridge (built near Ciudad del Este in 1964) also promoted trade in contraband. Smuggling of cheaper Paraguayan goods to Brazil and Argentina, and of stolen Brazilian goods into Paraguay, had been going on for a long time, but bigger populations along the border made this even more attractive. All this rapid development attracted Paraguayan small farmers from the overcrowded area near Asunción as well as farmers from Brazil and as far away as Japan. Unfortunately, the boom years came to an end in 1982 with the completion of the Itaipú Dam.

Itaipú is a dam across the Paraná River, which is the second-biggest river in South America (the biggest is the Amazon). Paraguay and Brazil agreed to build the dam together. Because Paraguay did not have enough money to pay its half of the $20 billion that it cost, Brazil paid for Paraguay on the understanding that Paraguay would sell a lot of its share of the electricity to Brazil at a reduced rate.

Construction began in 1975 and employed forty thousand workers in round-the-clock shifts to build the dam as fast as possible. Whole new industries grew up to supply the workers with cement to build the dam. It is estimated that 141 million cubic feet (4 million cubic meters) of concrete were poured into this huge dam. When the river was dammed, it created a reservoir that extended 100 miles (161 km) upstream and flooded the large Guairá waterfall. It was officially completed and open in 1982.

Itaipú is now the world's largest dam in generating capacity. It supplies 86 percent of the energy consumed by Paraguay and 15 percent of that consumed by Brazil. In July 2009, Brazil and Paraguay reached an agreement under which Brazil pays more to Paraguay for electricity from the Itaipú hydroelectric power plant and provides cheap loans for infrastructure. Brazil's concessions to Paraguay include a tripling of the fee it pays for access to about 90 percent of Paraguay's half-share of the energy produced at Itaipú, increasing the payment to $360 million a year.

In 2016, the dam achieved a generating record of 103 million megawatt-hours (MWh).

CURRENT ECONOMY

In the twenty-first century, agricultural production in Paraguay has soared, and Paraguay is now the fifth-largest soybean producer in the world. Many individuals living in the country make money through subsistence farming. More than one-fourth of the workforce is in the agricultural industry. Popular crops include cotton, sugarcane, soybeans, corn, and wheat. Pork, beef, and eggs are also favored agricultural products. For a time in 2012, there was concern about beef production with a rise in hoof-and-mouth disease, but that has cleared and the country is once again thriving from agricultural exports. The country's main exports include soybeans, livestock feed, cotton, meat, wood, leather, and gold. Since 2014, its economy has been growing at a rate of 4 percent per year.

Reforms in fiscal and monetary policy also have improved Paraguay's economy. Inflation has dropped, and the currency—called the guaraní—has appreciated, or gained, in value. Paraguay has the economic advantages of a young population and vast hydroelectric power, but it has few mineral resources, and chronic political instability has undercut some of the economic advantages present. The government welcomes foreign investment but historically has been unable to provide a stable, corruption-free environment for businesses. Smuggling and a large black market have deterred many foreign investors from entering the Paraguayan market.

Despite economic progress in some areas, Paraguay is still a developing country. It ranks as the third-poorest country in South America, with a 2017 gross domestic product (GDP) per capita of $9,800. Many people suffer in poverty—with 22 percent living below the poverty line.

AREAS OF THE ECONOMY

The agricultural sector is still the primary employer in Paraguay. About 26.5 percent of the labor force is engaged in farming, either for subsistence or export. Agriculture accounts for about 17.9 percent of Paraguay's GDP. The main export crops are soybeans, cotton, sugarcane, corn, and wheat. Paraguay also exports wood and livestock, such as cattle and pigs. Likewise, Paraguay is now the sixth-largest exporter of beef in the world.

The next biggest employer is industry, which includes mining, manufacturing, construction, and energy. In total, about 18.5 percent of people work in industry jobs. Mining makes up a small component of the economy. Renewable energy, especially hydroelectric energy, has become popular in the twenty-first century. The Yacyretá hydroelectric project between Paraguay and Argentina reached its full capacity in 2011, augmenting Paraguay's hydropower resources beyond the Itaipú Dam. Meanwhile, a renewable energy law was proposed in 2017 requiring the country's main energy supplier to commit 5 percent of its output to renewable sources other than hydroelectric power. Today, the country exports large amounts of its renewable energy to surrounding countries in the form of electricity. In fact, Paraguay is one of the world's largest electricity net exporters. In the country itself, 99.3 percent of electricity comes from hydroelectric power.

Because of the dominance of hydroelectricity, tariffs (mostly residential) are remarkably below the average for the region. Paraguay has no oil reserves; it relies on imported oil to meet its limited need for oil-produced energy.

The service sector has grown by leaps and bounds and employed 55 percent of Paraguay's working population as of 2008. This sector includes transportation, hotels, real estate, communication, restaurants, and financial services such as banking. The importation of goods, especially from Argentina and Brazil, for sale and illegal re-exportation creates service industry jobs. Instability in the economy and a large black market has hampered development of the formal services sector in Paraguay. However, advances are being made, as the tourism sector gradually grows.

IMPORTS AND EXPORTS

Trade is a vital source of government revenue through the collection of taxes imposed on imports. Paraguay's main trading partners are Brazil, Argentina, Chile, Russia, the United States, and China. Paraguay's main exports are agricultural products such as soybeans and cotton, and processed products

In 2010, it was discovered that Paraguay had one of the world's largest titanium ore deposits.

Ciudad del Este is the second-largest city in Paraguay.

such as edible oils and wood products. Paraguay is also a net exporter of electricity. Its main imports are electrical machinery, tractors, cars, vehicle parts, petroleum products, household appliances, tobacco, and chemicals.

One problem that has plagued trade relations between Paraguay, the United States, Argentina, and Brazil is smuggling. This is where people bring goods across the border without declaring them to the authorities and, hence, without paying taxes on them. Landlocked and one of the least-developed countries of South America, Paraguay has historically been a haven for smugglers tempted by the high tariffs systems of neighboring "giants" Argentina and Brazil. Ciudad del Este, where the boundaries of Paraguay, Brazil, and Argentina merge, has been a center for money laundering and drug smuggling. Other border areas, where law enforcement is weak, have also been hotbeds for these activities.

In 2007, Brazil confirmed plans for the construction of a steel and concrete wall along the Paraguayan border to help combat contraband—to stop smugglers from buying cheap imported goods in Paraguay and selling them in big Brazilian cities such as São Paulo. However, construction of the wall was not completed as of 2018.

AGRICULTURAL WORKERS

As of 2011, Ciudad del Este was home to the world's largest stolen car market.

Agricultural laborers make up over one-fourth of Paraguay's labor force. In Paraguay's early history, there was more land than there were people to farm it. Various governments encouraged farmers from other countries to settle in Paraguay and work the land. As the rural population grew, education and access to government services were neglected. Most rural people were poor, but as long as there was land to grow their own food, they survived. Stroessner changed this dramatically.

In the last twenty years of Stroessner's rule, he decided to develop large-scale farming, since only big farms efficiently produced enough cotton, cattle, or soybeans for export. A small farmer usually devoted most of his land to growing his own food and only a little to growing produce for sale. Such farmers made up the bulk of Paraguay's population. To reorganize the country for large-scale production, Stroessner expelled the peasants from their land and sold it to his wealthy friends for development.

By the 1990s, the rural situation was critical. Landless farmers started squatting on land to make a living. Many peasants moved into the cities in the hope of finding work. However, when there was high unemployment in the cities, workers had no recourse to family farms that once provided sustenance. Until 1982, 57 percent of Paraguayans lived in the countryside; ten years later, the majority (51 percent) lived in cities. Heavy country-to-city migration placed a great burden on the state. Often uneducated and untrained for urban work, peasants ended up doing part-time or illegal work. This was a problem across Latin America but was especially so in Paraguay, where the state had little money to help these people survive and too small an industrial sector to employ them. In many ways, this is still the case today.

EXPLOITATION OF THE LAND

The idea that land is inexhaustible has guided government programs since independence. Policies based on this erroneous assumption have brought Paraguay to a critical point. Similarly, the indigenous people, though a relatively small group, face social and economic crisis as a result of policies that have not heeded ecological issues.

Human use of the land can be divided as follows: the central zone around Asunción, the eastern zone farther from Asunción but still east of the Paraguay River, and the Chaco. The central zone has been settled for the longest time and has the highest population density. Some indigenous groups live in the eastern zone, which has seen increased settlement since the 1970s. The Chaco

Poverty and income inequality remain high, but between 2003 and 2016, the number of Paraguayans living on less than $5.50 US per day dropped by half as a result of economic growth.

A Paraguayan soybean farmer tends his field.

has been underpopulated for most of its history. Only 2 percent of Paraguay's population lives there. Most people living in the Chaco are cattle farmers.

As a result of more people farming the Chaco in the twenty-first century, the forests are nearly gone. In this region, many farms are too small for people to make a living. This leads to methods of farming that deplete the soil. Land is farmed every year without fertilizers, which are too costly; the soil becomes exhausted; and the crop yield diminishes. On bigger farms, owners are not concerned about protecting the soil because they have so much of it. Again the soil is worked to exhaustion. Other factors such as drought have also affected farming in this area and elsewhere in Paraguay.

Paraguay depends on farming and forestry for a large proportion of its exports. If forests continue to be harvested without a policy of replacement, there will be no trees left to exploit. Because better farming methods are not being promoted, the soil becomes depleted and yields decrease. Each year, the same piece of land produces less and less cotton or soybeans.

Finally, Paraguay's indigenous people have been losing their land continually since the 1960s with little government intervention. Large land-owning companies have been destroying their lands and forests with bulldozers and other machinery. Without land, they are forced to change the way they live and their culture. When this happens to people, they often lose their will to live and turn to self-abuse, using drugs and alcohol, or commit suicide. The ecological crisis affects not only the soil or the number of trees; it is also a social problem.

It was estimated that Paraguay exported more than $11 billion worth of goods around the world in 2017, including soybeans, corn, and beef. Inflation has dropped, and the currency has appreciated. However, unequal land distribution has resulted in a large class of peasant farm laborers. A big portion of the population is uninvolved in the formal economy, instead existing as subsistence farmers.

Paraguay voted in favor of the UN Declaration on the Rights of Indigenous Peoples in 2007, which acknowledged human rights for people from native communities. However, the country's indigenous population continues to experience discrimination and violation of their rights.

INTERNET LINKS

http://www.focus-economics.com/countries/paraguay
This website contains economic information about Paraguay.

http://www.itaipu.gov.br/en
Visit the official web page for Itaipú Binacional, the corporation that runs the Itaipú hydroelectric plant.

ENVIRONMENT

This aerial view shows the devastating deforestation in the Chaco.

5

PARAGUAY'S FORESTS OFFER GREAT potential for an abundance of wildlife. Today, many unique species can be found in Paraguay. However, major environmental threats such as deforestation, mining, and pollution worsen every day.

MAKING ROOM FOR FARMLAND

Agricultural expansion poses a major threat to the environment in Paraguay. In particular, production of soybeans and cotton has soared, and most of these crops are exported. Beef and soy production are major causes of deforestation. A great deal of the rain forest in the east has been destroyed for agricultural purposes, particularly soy and wheat crops, as well as cattle ranching. As of 2017, Paraguay had the sixth-highest deforestation rate in the world as a direct result of increased ranching and agriculture. The absence of trees contributes to the loss of soil through erosion. This could ultimately lead to unsuccessful farming in the region itself and landslides.

Steps to protect certain parts of the country from deforestation have been taken in the twenty-first century. The 2004 Zero Deforestation Law passed by Duarte's government successfully slowed deforestation in the eastern part of the country by 90 percent. However, the law applied only to eastern Paraguay, ignoring the Chaco, which is still experiencing rapid deforestation. This law was due to expire in December 2013, but the government chose to extend it to 2018.

RIVERS

Sources of water pollution include industrial pollutants and sewage. Many of the country's rivers suffer from toxic dumping. Tanneries, or factories where animal hides are lightened with chemicals, are particularly harmful, releasing mercury and chromium into rivers and streams. Runoff from toxic chemicals and fertilizers used by farmers—particularly soy farmers—also seeps into Paraguay's waters. However, access to clean water has increased a great deal in recent years. Today, 98 percent of people living in Paraguay have access to clean water.

In addition to pollution, climate change has had a negative impact on Paraguay's rivers. Many areas of the Pilcomayo River have been drying out due to drought. This has caused large numbers of caimans, fish, and other animals to die. Up to 98 percent of caimans and 80 percent of capybaras in some parts of the river have disappeared.

DISPOSAL OF WASTE

Problems of sanitation have plagued Paraguay in the twenty-first century and have prompted action from the government. In 2006, the government declared a health emergency when the two obsolete incinerators that disposed of the waste generated by Asunción's public hospitals were closed down. That coincided with the city government's decision to cancel the contract with the Sudamericana Company, which was in charge of collecting and incinerating the waste from private hospitals in the capital, after authorities found that it was not complying with the requirements set by the local government. The accumulation of waste reached levels incompatible with minimal hygiene standards, to the point that scheduled surgical operations had to be canceled for fear of the spread of hospital infections. Given the lack of other means of disposing of hospital waste, collection was suspended for nearly two months.

In 2007, the government assumed responsibility for all sanitation matters under the Ministry of Public Works and Communications. Over the next seven years, substantial progress was made. By 2014, sanitation conditions had improved by 84 percent.

ENVIRONMENTAL PROTECTION

Agencies responsible for environmental protection within Paraguay include the National Environmental Health Service, the Ministry of Public Health, and the Ministry of Public Works and Communications. In the twenty-first century, more action has been taken to protect the environment, although more could still be done.

Genetically modified soybean crops are treated with chemicals.

In 2001, the Inter-American Development Bank (IDB) approved an $8 million loan to improve and strengthen the environmental sector in Paraguay. This was a two-step process, with the second step being enacted in June 2008. The first step established a framework for managing environmental materials. The second step, kicked off by another $8 million loan, developed a National Environmental System in Paraguay, and worked to educate and engage citizens in environmental management.

In 2013, the World Bank partnered with Itaipú on the Paraguay Biodiversity Project, which was implemented to combat deforestation by restoring protected land, increasing conservation efforts, and reducing water pollution.

In 2015, Paraguay signed the Paris Climate Agreement, a global initiative to reduce harmful pollution emission levels. It is among nearly 200 countries to commit to the program. Paraguay's allegiance means that, starting in 2020, it will take specific measures to limit its carbon footprint, such as reducing the amount of factories or vehicles in the country. Other environmental preservation efforts will also be enacted during that time.

In March 2018, Paraguay signed a declaration with Brazil and Bolivia calling for conservation of the tropical wetland areas shared by the three countries. This would help save crucial habitats for species living there.

GENETICALLY MODIFED SOY

The Chaco is an arid region that has seen great deforestation in the twenty-first century. Likewise, for the 2 percent of people living there, the area has been a place where farming has become a main industry. Cattle farming is most popular; however, soybean farming is also trying to gain a foothold.

Paraguay is among the world's top exporters of genetically modified (GM) soy. GM soy is exported to many places, including Europe and China, where it is used to feed animals and to produce biodiesel for cars. Many fear that GM products like soy could be bad for the environment. Despite that, GM soy continues to be grown in places around the world, especially Paraguay. In 2018, Paraguay topped Argentina for soybeans exportation. Today, 3 percent of the world's soybean exports come from Paraguay.

While this is good for the economy, soy is the second-largest cause of deforestation around the world, second only to beef. Since soy is used as animal feed, soy production increases as beef consumption rises. In Paraguay, soy farming has led to over-harvesting of forests. In the Chaco, this is particularly bad. Likewise, the industry of land clearing has brought farmers from neighboring countries to do the work. This has led indigenous and smaller farmers in Paraguay to lose their land or face competition. In some instances, this has widened the wealth gap in the country.

ACCESS TO CLEAN WATER

Responsibility for water and sanitation service provision in Paraguay in urban areas rests primarily with the Ministry of Public Works and Communications. It oversees nearly 2,500 community-managed water associations (Juntas de Saneamiento) in small cities and in rural areas. The national enterprise, the Empresa de Servicios Sanitarios de Paraguay (ESSAP), is responsible for serving communities with populations of more than ten thousand inhabitants. It has a particular presence in Asunción. In rural communities and small towns with fewer than ten thousand inhabitants, water associations provide services, while technical assistance and financing are provided by the National Environmental Sanitation Service (SENASA).

A fascinating phenomenon in Paraguay is the presence of independent private water suppliers, called *aguateros*, since the 1970s. Their efforts account for a significant share of the expansion of urban water coverage in the area of the capital. *Aguateros* are private, informal service providers that operate small-scale water systems. In 2017, *aguateros* were advocating for expanding

The Cateura landfill, located near Asunción, services the people in the greater Asunción area. It has about five hundred gancheros, or recyclers, working there. Every day, men, women, and children sift through the 1.6 tons (1.5 metric tons) of waste deposited daily. Some materials are organic and

biodegradable, others are inorganic and exposed to diseases that come from bacteria and toxic waste. Working on the landfill, gancheros, named after the large hook (or gancho in Spanish) of their garbage-separating poles, undertake back-breaking work recycling amid the most difficult, subhuman conditions.

They are trained in recycling techniques and often sell their finds for pennies a day. However, through these efforts, a curious organization has materialized. In 2006, a sanitation worker and music instructor named Favio Chávez realized there could be real treasure found in the trash collected at the landfill. It started after he brought the orchestra he teaches to play for the gancheros at Cateura. Some of those who attended the concert were inspired by what they heard. They asked Chávez if he could teach their children to play instruments. Chávez knew the parents couldn't afford them, so he decided to fashion his own instruments out of the garbage around him.

Today, Chávez teaches Paraguay's only recycling and landfill orchestra. Thirty kids make up the orchestra. Each plays an instrument made from recycled materials. They have gained international recognition and have traveled around the world to play in countries such as the United States, Canada, Norway, and Japan. Exposure to music has given the children hope and aspirations to pursue music or other performance professions.

The spider flower is one of thousands of plant species in Paraguay.

their services to other parts of the country, but cited the government as blocking their efforts.

A 2007 law passed in Paraguay declared that access to clean drinking water was a basic human right. This led to an increase in the number of water associations established. On April 14, 2009, the World Bank approved a $64 million loan for the Paraguay Water and Sanitation Sector Modernization Project. The objective of the project was to increase the efficiency, coverage, and sustainability of water supply and sanitation services in Paraguay. The project expanded drinking water services in rural areas, including for indigenous communities, by building new water supply systems and remodeling existing ones. Access to clean water has improved in recent years, with 98 percent of city dwellers and 94 percent of rural people now with access to pure drinking water.

PARAGUAYAN PLANTS

There are about seven thousand species of plants in Paraguay, of which more than two-thirds are found in the eastern part of the country. This rich flora has been attributed to the mosaic of habitat types in the country and the position of Paraguay at the edge of the tropics. Sadly, many of these species are endangered.

Some examples of popular plants and trees in Paraugay are palm trees, urunday, *peterebi*, *samuú*, medicinal plants, and stevia plants used to make low-calorie sweeteners.

PARAGUAY'S FRAGILE ANIMALS

Paraguay is home to many diverse animals. Mammals, fish, and birds are the most common. Many of them live in forests or wetlands. Common sights include parrots, marsh deer, monkeys, armadillos, and wild boar. However, there are animals that face extinction as well.

PILAR TUCO-TUCO   The tuco-tucos are members of a group of rodents that can all be found in South America. Tuco-tucos are heavily built with short

Part of the Guaraní Aquifer, the world's second-largest underground freshwater reserve, sits beneath Paraguay. It is estimated to be capable of providing the world with drinking water for up to two hundred years.

legs. Their skin is loose, possibly so they can slide through the tunnels they create. They have long forefeet for burrowing and bristled hind feet for grooming. They have large heads, small ears, and hairy tails. Their body ranges in size from 5.9 to 9.8 inches (15 to 25 cm) in length, and they can weigh up to 25 ounces (700 grams). The Pilar tuco-tuco, native to Paraguay, is an endangered species, and its numbers continue to decrease.

The rare giant otter can be seen in the Paraguay River.

COATIMUNDI Coatimundis, or coatis (*coatimundi* is the Guaraní name for these animals), are members of the raccoon family. Adult coatis measure 13 to 27 inches (33 to 69 cm) and weigh between 6 and 18 pounds (between 3 and 8 kg), about the size of a large housecat. Males can become almost twice as large as females and have large, sharp canine teeth.

All coatis have a slender head with an elongated, flexible, slightly upward-turned nose, small ears, dark feet, and a long tail used for balance and signaling. Coatis have bear- and raccoon-like paws and walk on the soles of their feet, like human beings. They have strong limbs for climbing and digging, and have a reputation for intelligence, like the raccoon. Unfortunately, coatis face unregulated hunting and the serious threat of environmental destruction in Central and South America.

GIANT OTTER The giant otter is a carnivorous mammal that ranges across north-central South America. Males are between 4.9 and 5.9 feet (1.5 and 1.8 m) in length and females are between 4.9 and 5.6 feet (1.5 and 1.7 m). The animal's well-muscled tail can account for as much as 27 inches (69 cm) of total body length. Weights are between 70 and 100 pounds (32 and 45 kg) for males and 48 and 57 pounds (22 and 26 kg) for females. Decades of being poached for their velvety pelt, peaking in the 1950s and 1960s, have hugely diminished the number of giant otters. They are among the most endangered species in Paraguay. Their way of life continues to be threatened as agricultural development and deforestation persist. Efforts to educate the population about the importance of the giant otter and other critical animals are ongoing in the country. However, illegal trade and hunting continually lowers their numbers in the wild as well.

Endangered species in Paraguay include the Chacoan peccary, the giant otter, and the Pilar tuco-tuco. Many other species are considered vulnerable or threatened, such as the giant anteater and the jaguar.

PROTECTED PARKS

Despite great amounts of deforestation occurring, efforts to preserve and protect certain sections of the country's natural elements have resulted in the creation of parks and wildlife reserves.

MBARACAYÚ NATURE RESERVE   Mbaracayú, located in the eastern region of Paraguay, protects 172,973 acres (70,000 hectares) of Paraguay's Interior Atlantic Forest, a highly threatened ecoregion that once covered large parts of Paraguay, Brazil, and Argentina. Today, its presence has been severely reduced in size. Less than 2 percent of the forest remains in Paraguay.

Paraguay's section was established to conserve the unique biodiversity of flora and fauna within the Paraguayan reserve system. Today, Mbaracayú is one of the largest remaining tracts of privately owned dense humid subtropical forest in South America. It has over two thousand species living there, some endemic and endangered.

Organizations such as the World Wildlife Fund are establishing educational and preservation projects within the Atlantic Forest, in Brazil and Paraguay, bringing with them knowledge of how to preserve some truly amazing natural wonders.

DEFENSORES DEL CHACO NATIONAL PARK   Defensores del Chaco National Park is located in the heart of the Paraguayan Chaco. It protects one of the very few seasonal freshwater springs that supplies vital drinking water to the western Chaco region. It also lies within the Chaco Biosphere Reserve, an area whose UNESCO designation further protects the wildlife there.

Chaco is home to many endemic and endangered species, including many mammal species that are not as well represented in neighboring ecoregions. Jaguars are some of the most elusive creatures, but they are said to have a presence in the park as well as the Gran Chaco area. Conservation efforts to protect the jaguar in particular have been made in the twenty-first century. The Chaco Jaguar Conservation Project aims to educate others and monitor jaguar movements in the Chaco park and the greater Chaco region. Likewise, it hopes to create a genetic reference library to combat illegal killing and trading

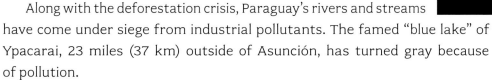

GOODBYE, CERRO LEÓN?

In 2015, there were proposals to blow up Cerro León, the highest mountain in the Chaco. The official reason was to supply rock for paving roads, but it may also have been due to rumors that the mountain contains uranium. Cerro León holds religious significance for the Guaraní in addition to being a major attraction of Defensores del Chaco National Park. Fortunately, public outcry and demonstrations halted the plans.

of jaguars. Deforestation and human-jaguar conflicts are the greatest threats to the animals today.

ÑACUNDAY NATIONAL PARK   This park sits on 4,942 acres (2,000 ha) of land and harbors a part of Paraguay's Atlantic Forest. It is the site of natural beauty, including the Salto Ñacunday, the most important waterfall in the country. The park also has much wildlife and plant life living within it. Examples include the Ñacunda nighthawk, orchids, monkeys, foxes, and otters.

Along with the deforestation crisis, Paraguay's rivers and streams have come under siege from industrial pollutants. The famed "blue lake" of Ypacarai, 23 miles (37 km) outside of Asunción, has turned gray because of pollution.

While there have been several fronts to preserve Paraguay's environment, there is still much more to do to make that a reality.

The Salto Ñacunday is a waterfall in the Ñacunday National Park.

INTERNET LINKS

https://ptes.org/grants/worldwide-projects/jaguars-in-paraguay
Read about the jaguar's precarious state in Paraguay and efforts being taken to help protect it.

https://www.worldwildlife.org
Visit the official website of the World Wildlife Fund, which helps protect and conserve wildlife around the planet.

PARAGUAYANS

A Paraguayan family enjoys a meal of traditional foods together.

PARAGUAYANS ARE UNIQUE AMONG the peoples of South America. Most live in urban areas, are poor, and have a single ethnic background. Paraguay ranks as the third-poorest country in South America, with a 2017 GDP per capita of $9,800. Paraguay's poverty rate has declined in recent years but is still high, particularly in rural areas. About one-quarter of the population lives below the poverty line.

6

The majority of Paraguayans are mestizos, or of mixed native and European heritage. Other groups include Africans, Japanese, indigenous people, Mennonites, Chinese, Koreans, and Brazilians.

ETHNICITIES

In the early exploration years, there were few Spaniards in Paraguay because of the absence of mineral wealth, such as gold, and large indigenous societies whose labor could be exploited. Some Spaniards who explored and later settled in the region married the local Guaraní and adapted to their way of life.

Today, Paraguay is one of the most homogeneous countries in South America. Most people are of the same ethnicity—mestizo, or descendants of those first marriages between Spaniards and Guaraní during the early colonial period. About 95 percent of the modern population of Paraguay is made up of this group, and their primary languages are Guaraní and Spanish.

The German-speaking Mennonites maintain their cultural identity in Paraguay.

The remaining 5 percent of the population is an interesting mixture of ethnic groups. They include people of African descent, estimated at 1 percent of the population, whose ancestors were slaves brought to Paraguay beginning in colonial times. They were absorbed into the mestizo and Guaraní populations through intermarriage, and many of them are not easily distinguishable from the majority in appearance or language.

Other groups began arriving after the War of the Triple Alliance. More than half of the total population was killed in that war, so successive governments wooed migrants from abroad to repopulate the country. Between 1882 and 1907, about twelve thousand immigrants arrived in Asunción. Three-quarters were from Europe, mainly Italy, Germany, France, and Spain. The rest came from neighboring countries and from the Middle East. Most of them joined urban trades and commerce and became the core of the middle class.

In the twentieth century, through joint agreements between Paraguay and Japan, Japanese farmers established agricultural colonies near Asunción and Encarnación. Today, there is a steady population of Japanese people in Paraguay. The Japanese have learned Spanish and Guaraní to communicate with their neighbors, but they generally have not intermarried with mestizos due to harsh bias that has persisted through generations.

Another group that has remained largely separate from the majority is the German-speaking Mennonites. They began to settle in the Chaco region in the 1920s and 1930s. The first Mennonite groups to arrive were from Canada; they immigrated because the Canadian government tried to replace German with English as the language of instruction in Mennonite schools. The majority of Mennonite communities originated in Germany and spoke and taught in German, up until after World War II. Today, Mennonite communities still practice German but also speak a country's official language(s), depending on where they live. Subsequent groups of Mennonites came from the Soviet Union in the 1940s, fleeing religious persecution there. Today, the majority of Mennonites live in the Chaco region. Other smaller communities live in the eastern region. In the twenty-first century, Mennonite colonies there have been responsible for an increasing percentage of Paraguay's dairy and beef production.

IMMIGRATION

In terms of immigration, in the twentieth century people were coming from countries such as Germany, Korea, China, and Brazil. They settled throughout Paraguay, taking advantage of loose immigration policies and exciting developmental projects such as dams. In the twenty-first century, however, fewer people have immigrated to the region. Instead, many people have left the country. That is because better opportunities have presented themselves in places like Canada and the United States. Today, large amounts of people continue to leave Paraguay, despite efforts to draw others to the country through business partnerships and a budding tourism industry. Corruption and violence also contribute to an exodus of Paraguayan citizens.

Here, men of the Aché indigenous people are shown at archery practice. Each man holds a bow.

INDIGENOUS PEOPLES

According to the 2012 National Census of Population and Housing for Indigenous Peoples, 2 percent of Paraguay's population is indigenous. These people belong to nineteen different ethnic groups, including Chulupi, Aché, Lengua, and Macá. The majority of the groups lives in the Chaco and speaks four different languages, while the groups living in eastern Paraguay speak variations of Guaraní. Their way of life has survived in the twentieth and twenty-first centuries because they tend to live far from the most settled region around Asunción.

The existence of indigenous people living in the eastern forests was severely threatened when the government actively began promoting development in the region in the 1970s. Indigenous people were forcibly removed from their land when new settlers arrived.

The Chaco groups west of the Paraguay River were once even more isolated. But they were caught up in the Chaco War and often used as scouts by both

Members of the Sawhoyamaxa community are seen in Villa Hayes in 2013, before the return of their lands.

the Bolivian and the Paraguayan armies. They also lost land to Mennonite settlers and large ranching concerns that invaded the region before and after the war. Because many of the Chaco natives were primarily hunters and gatherers, they were negatively affected when ranchers started fencing off the land and prohibiting them from using it.

Despite having pride in their Guaraní heritage and language, many Paraguayans have negative feelings toward the country's remaining indigenous groups. In the 2010s, the small ethnic indigenous community has made stands against the government, which has been accused of violating their basic human rights. The indigenous people of Paraguay have been denied medicine, wages, and shelter, and they suffer from malnutrition and disease. Many people in indigenous communities live in poverty.

Land rights continue to be a concern to indigenous communities. However, in recent years, several indigenous communities have had their land returned to them after lengthy legal battles. These groups include the Yakye Axa in 2012, the Sawhoyamaxa in 2014, and most recently, the Xákmok Kásek in 2017. The Xákmok Kásek were forced out of their territory by ranching companies over thirty years ago, causing many members of the community to die as a result of extreme poverty. In January 2017, the Paraguayan government returned 72 percent of this group's ancestral lands.

MIGRATION

Paraguay was a predominantly rural country for a long time. Since the 1960s, however, there has been internal and external migration. Internally, the pattern was more urbanization, with rural people moving into cities or larger towns. Overcrowding in the agricultural zone around Asunción is partly responsible. Peasants have been forced off their land by large landowners and have had to go to Asunción or farther afield to find employment. When the Itaipú project started, there was a construction boom all over the country, and many rural poor were attracted to either Ciudad del Este in the east or to Asunción. As a result of these shifts, about 61.6 percent of the population lives in urban areas.

Another general trend in internal migration has been toward the eastern border with Brazil. There were several reasons: the Itaipú project created jobs, convenient road access via the Friendship Bridge increased trade with Brazil, and the government sold land in the area at a low price.

The area with the highest population density is Asunción, with 11,622 people per square mile (4,487 people per sq km). By comparison, the Chaco has less than 1 person per square mile (0.4 people per sq km). The population density has actually decreased in the Chaco despite an increase in Paraguay's overall population because of the deterioration of the environment in the region and a crippling drought. For the country as a whole, the population density averages out to 45 people per square mile (17 per sq km).

While many rural Paraguayans have migrated to the cities, many others have left to find work in Argentina, Uruguay, or Brazil. This is an ongoing trend, but one that has increased in modern times. Again, due to a lack of land in the central farming region, many men have been forced to seek work elsewhere. Many of them ended up in northeastern Argentina, on tobacco plantations or in the textile and lumber industries. Women mostly headed for Buenos Aires, where they worked as maids. Between 1955 and 1970, some 650,000 Paraguayans emigrated, mainly to Argentina.

Migrant workers tend to be young, which contributes to the fact that Paraguay's population has aged slightly on average. It is still a rather youthful population, with 24.5 percent of the people under the age of fifteen. Life expectancy in Paraguay has improved and is now 77.4 years. The birth rate has dropped significantly and is now 1.9 children per woman.

WEALTH INEQUALITY

Wealth and income distribution in Paraguay are extremely unequal. A small group of elite people owns most of the land and commercial wealth and has

The poverty level among Paraguay's indigenous peoples is far above the national average for the country. This is a result of systematic discrimination, expulsion from their lands, and general violation of their basic human rights by both the government and non-indigenous society.

reaped most of the benefits of economic growth in recent decades. Indigenous peoples are the most impoverished. Mennonite and Japanese immigrants have established thriving agricultural colonies, while Korean, Chinese, and Arab immigrant groups are concentrated in urban commercial activities and re-exportation. Brazilian immigrants are disproportionately concentrated in midsize commercial farming enterprises but also include extremely impoverished small farmers and laborers as well as wealthy landowners and middle-class entrepreneurs.

RIGHTS

Until the late twentieth century, the oppressed population was never well organized to fight for their rights. The splits in the Colorado Party in the 1980s and the conditions that led to this—Alfredo Stroessner's rule, the economic downturn and international isolation—provided an opportunity for demonstrations and statements by the opposition.

Liberal Party leader Domingo Laíno served as the focal point of the opposition in the second half of the 1980s. The government's effort to isolate Laíno by exiling him in 1982 had backfired. On his sixth attempt, in 1986, Laíno returned with three television crews from the United States, a former US ambassador to Paraguay, and a group of Uruguayan and Argentine congressmen. Laíno took the lead in organizing demonstrations and diminishing somewhat the normal opposition party infighting. The opposition held numerous lightning demonstrations, especially in rural areas. Such demonstrations were held and disbanded quickly before the arrival of the police. Opposition politicians also saw several encouraging developments. Some 53 percent of those polled indicated that there was "uneasiness" in Paraguayan society. Furthermore, 74 percent believed that the political situation needed changes, including 45 percent who wanted a substantial or total change. It would be two more decades after the 1988 general elections before the Paraguayan electorate would actually vote for total change in the form of Fernando Lugo in the 2008 elections. This change was short lived, however, since after Lugo's impeachment in 2012, the Colorado Party resumed control.

Today, as seen by actions taken by indigenous communities and other peoples in Paraguay, more people are fighting for their rights. More people are likewise voicing their opinions and exploring ways to make Paraguay a better country.

TRADITIONAL CLOTHING

Paraguayans have a rich cultural history. Much of this history can be reflected in their way of dressing.

Women perform the Paraguayan polka while dressed in traditional clothing.

Traditional dress, like so much else, provides echoes of a largely agrarian heritage. Men wear full trousers of brown, light gray, or bright blue fabric and a loose shirt open at the neck. Bandanas are tied loosely around their necks, and they wear flat-topped, cowboy-style hats, sometimes decorated with red, white, and blue (the national colors) flowers around the brim. To complete the outfit, there are leather boots, a striped poncho, and a wide cloth sash around the waist. Women's traditional dress is a full-pleated skirt worn with a white apron that is often decorated with lace. Under the skirt and showing below its hem, women wear big ruffled petticoats of white cotton. Their blouses are worn off the shoulder, and the sleeves are made of lace. The body of the blouse is often embroidered in red, white, and blue to match the men's hats. Their hair is worn up, and they wear jewelry of silver or coral.

This type of dress is no longer seen in the countryside, though tourists can see examples of it at folkloric performances. Most people wear mass-manufactured clothes made locally or imported. In the city, most people wear clothes seen being worn in any city in the Western world.

FAMOUS PARAGUAYANS

In modern times, there have been several Paraguayans to have a profound effect on the country.

FERNANDO LUGO   Fernando Armindo Lugo Méndez was born in 1951 in the village of San Solano, near the Brazilian border. Under Stroessner's dictatorship, Lugo's father was detained on twenty separate occasions, and three of Lugo's four brothers were forced to flee the country for their own safety. In 1977, he graduated from the Catholic University in Asunción and was ordained as a priest. Lugo then spent five years in Ecuador working with the poor, where he developed an interest in social justice. After returning to Paraguay, he was named a bishop by the Catholic Church in 1994. During his eleven years leading the diocese of San Pedro Apostol del Ycuamandiyú in one of the country's poorest regions, Lugo began working towards land reform to assist impoverished farmers.

Due to his work on land reform, a movement started with the goal of trying to get Lugo into elected office. Because members of the clergy were not allowed to hold office, Lugo requested to leave the priesthood. The Vatican rejected his request but allowed him to retire as bishop, which gave him the freedom to become more politically active. In 2007, Lugo joined a small political party that would eventually join with other small parties to form the Patriotic Alliance for Change coalition in time for the 2008 presidential election. He was chosen to run as their candidate, and he ran a campaign centered on social reform and an end to corruption, with the campaign slogan "Paraguay Para Todos" (Paraguay for Everybody). On April 20, 2008, Lugo defeated Blanca Ovelar of the Colorado Party to end sixty-one years of continuous Colorado rule. His swearing-in on August 15, 2008, was the first time in Paraguay's history that the party in charge peacefully handed the office over to the opposing party. Upon election, Lugo stated that he would refuse the presidential salary and encouraged other politicians to refuse theirs as well.

In 2009, Lugo's approval rate dropped after he was accused of fathering several children while still a bishop. In 2012, a land dispute resulting in the death of seventeen people also led to a speedy impeachment trial for Lugo. He was forced out of office on June 22, 2012. This led to protests by his supporters. In addition, several neighboring countries disapproved of the speed of his impeachment, questioning whether it was legal and calling it a coup by the opposing party. Ambassadors were recalled from Paraguay and the country was suspended from the Mercosur trade bloc and the Union of South American Nations until the next election, which was held in April 2013.

PAZ ENCINA   Director and film writer Paz Encina was born in Paraguay in 1971, at the height of Stroessner's dictatorship. She studied communication at the University of Asunción and went on to study film directing at the Universidad del Cine in Buenos Aires. Much of her work reflects the isolation and violence entrenched in Paraguay's history due to years of dictatorship and war. Encina directed a number of short films and video installations before directing her first feature film, *Hamaca Paraguaya* (Paraguayan Hammock) in 2006. This award-winning film takes place during the Chaco War. One of her short films is *Viento Sur* (A Wind from the South) from 2012. It is a dialogue between two brothers trying to figure out whether to survive Stroessner's troops through migration or armed opposition. Encina's most recent film is *Ejercicios de Memoria* (Memory Exercises), released in 2016. This film is the result of her research into the records kept by Stroessner's government. The characters in Encina's films speak a combination of Spanish and Guaraní.

This photo shows Paraguayan filmmaker Paz Encina.

INTERNET LINKS

https://www.festival-cannes.com/en/artist/paz-encina
Read this short biography about Paz Encina and her accomplishments in the film industry.

http://www.iwgia.org/en/paraguay
The website for the human rights organization International Work Group for Indigenous Affairs includes news and information about the indigenous peoples of Paraguay.

LIFESTYLE

Three Paraguayan girls pose on the steps of a local church.

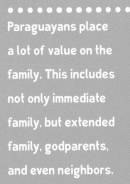

7

PARAGUAYANS OF ALL SOCIAL classes have one thing in common: the importance they place on family. People in Paraguay rely on family connections for nearly everything and show great respect for these relationships. In rural communities, they rely on their neighbors for help as well.

BLENDING OF CULTURES

The Paraguayan lifestyle is a blend of traditions from indigenous and European cultures. Spanish culture did not become dominant here, as it did in other Latin American countries, nor were native cultures all destroyed. In fact, the mestizos of Paraguay are as much products of their Guaraní ancestors as they are of their Spanish ancestors. The language of most homes is Guaraní, not Spanish, and many family traditions observed today are directly related to Guaraní social customs. The Spaniards did not so much conquer Paraguay as blend in with its largest cultural group, the Guaraní.

PATRONES AND *PEONES*

The differences between rural and urban Paraguay have become more marked in the twentieth and twenty-first centuries. Until about fifty years ago, almost everyone lived in the countryside. Most of what we identify as particularly Paraguayan has its roots in their mestizo and rural past. These two facts of history have shaped modern culture more than anything else.

Before there was excessive competition for farmland, peasants (small farmers) moved around cultivating free land wherever they found it. Like their Guaraní ancestors, they used slash-and-burn cultivation. When yields decreased from soil exhaustion, the farmer would move to another area.

Most people with small holdings did not have formal title to or ownership of their land. Since they were mostly nomadic, they did not bother applying for ownership, or they could not get it, even if they wanted to, because they were farming land belonging to a larger estate.

In the latter case, relations between the peasants and landowners were well defined, though actual rights to the land were not. The large landowner was known as a *patron* (pah-TRON), while the peasant was called the *peon* (pay-OHN). *Patron-peon* relations were set by custom rather than by law. The *patron* allowed the *peon* to farm on his land in return for occasional gifts of produce on the *patron*'s birthday or at harvest time. Sometimes the *patron* demanded labor from the *peon*. This was never done directly, but followed a pattern of etiquette. The *patron* suggested that he needed a favor; the *peon* responded that he would be glad to help. Relations were never put into hard terms. There was no preset price in goods or labor, just customary relations of favors and gifts.

Beyond the economic sphere, *patrones* were also supposed to help *peones* during crises. When a *peon*'s family member died, for instance, the *patron* was expected to help with funeral costs. When the *peon* had trouble with the law, the *patron* acted as his protector. In return, the *peon* owed the *patron* loyalty. In politics, this meant that the *peon* was expected to support candidates the *patron* favored. These ties lasted for generations. Interestingly, such long-term loyalty between poorer and wealthier people carried over into other realms. People often patronized only one storekeeper, even when the competition offered better prices. In return, storekeepers gave loyal customers special deals. Paraguayans still relate to one another in this way.

There were also customary relations between neighbors. They helped one another at harvest or planting time, and once again, the relationship was never formalized. No one paid a neighbor for his work, but they knew that they owed him a favor at some later date. This type of relationship cemented a community together.

EXPANDING

Small villages scattered along the dirt roads linking farms were collections of essential services like the general store and the church. The most common form of transportation in isolated regions was the ox-drawn cart. This way of transporting items is still seen today in some communities.

With so few paved roads, cars and trucks were impractical. Local craftspeople, teachers, and government officials lived in town, and a few peasants made a living as domestic servants for these people. Other than for festivals or essential commercial transactions, peasants did not come to town regularly. Larger landowners also maintained residences in town, and townspeople were considered socially superior to country dwellers.

Much of this changed in the mid to late 1900s, with increasing competition for land. As more and more peasants started using the land of large landowners, the latter pressured the government to force the peasants to move away. This

Here you can see the unpaved streets of the town of Coronel Bogado.

was the beginning of the slow trickle of peasants into the cities and to the forested areas in the east.

Today, there are a variety of ways to transport people and items in Paraguay. In the cities, people typically drive cars or carts, walk, or take public transportation in the form of buses. Due to inconsistency of paved roadways, travel can take quite a long time in Paraguay. In the countryside, ox-drawn carts and trucks are mostly ways to get from place to place. Trucks are especially useful in navigating muddy roads, if the area should receive large amounts of rain. Paraguay also depends on rail systems, rivers, semi trucks, and airplanes to transport items internationally. As of 2013, there were nearly eight hundred airports in the country, but only fifteen of them had paved runways. The largest airports are Silvio Pettirossi International and Guaraní International. Each year, over four hundred thousand people travel by air.

IMPORTANCE OF FAMILY

Family ties, even if distant, have traditionally been far more important than any other type of association in Paraguay. People depend on family connections for almost anything they need, from help finding work to money and favors. This is one fact of life that does not distinguish rich from poor or urban from rural: everyone places a great deal of importance and respect on family relationships.

Guaraní heritage is also apparent because there is slightly more emphasis on maternal relatives. From the earliest mixed marriages, the mothers had more kin connections since the fathers were from Spain and arrived alone. This tradition of looking to the mother's relatives continues to the present.

The typical household is the nuclear family—mother, father, and their unmarried children, who usually stay home until they marry and sometimes return in the event of a divorce. The birth rate has changed in the twenty-first century. As of 2018, the average age of a woman when she had her first child was twenty-three. A typical household has no more than two children. Use of contraceptives is contributing to lower numbers of children per family.

Traditionally, the man is the acknowledged head of the household, and the woman takes care of the children and manages the finances. She maintains close ties with her own kin. If she works, she is still the primary caretaker of

GODPARENTS AND ADOPTION

Since their ideal is to have many relatives to turn to in case of need, Paraguayans have invented ways to expand their family circle by including nonrelations or by changing distant relatives into closer ones through fictive ties. There are two ways to do this: godparenthood and adoption.

At the time a child is baptized, the parents nominate two other people, usually a married couple, to be the child's godparents. In Paraguay, the godparents have quite a lot to do with the child as he or she grows up. Parents choose godparents very carefully, and usually they seek people who are better off than themselves in the hope that the godparents will be able to help with expenses like education or health care throughout the child's life. In return, the child is expected to show loyalty to the godparents and help them should they request it.

People can also invent or change their kin relationships through adoption. The usual pattern is for wealthier urban families, related or not, to adopt a poor child from the countryside. This could be fairly informal, or it may be made legal. Adopted children were either those born to unwed poor mothers or into families already too big to support them. This is viewed as one way that relatives, no matter how distant, can help each other.

the children and domestic duties. The man socializes mostly outside the home. This is the traditional pattern.

There are some single-parent households, usually headed by the mother and the result of a divorce. In these households, the woman lives alone with her children. After a divorce, children remain with their mother, while their father remarries or lives with his parents. There is little legal pressure for him to pay support. This is why households headed by women are among the poorest. There are few single-adult households, partly because few people can afford this and most prefer to live with relatives.

MARRIAGE

There are three types of marriage in Paraguay: civil, religious, and consensual. The first involves acquiring a license from the state and having a ceremony with a small celebration. The second, a traditional church wedding, is usually

In a society focused on family and ties to a mother's relatives, it is odd that women's rights have low currency in Paraguay. In the twenty-first century, women have established roles as both hard workers outside of the home and child-rearers. It seems, however, that in the public sphere they continue to be treated as second-class citizens.

Despite this, some women stand out as committed to change. The first woman to graduate as a lawyer (in 1907) was Serafina Dávalos. Her thesis, entitled "Humanism," was rediscovered by modern feminists in the 1980s. It outlines women's position in different social and economic levels, and proposes radical changes to address the inequalities she witnessed.

Others worked toward suffrage throughout the early to mid 1900s. In 1963, women finally won the right to vote. In 1989, Andrés Rodríguez's cabinet included the first female minister, Dr. Cynthia Prieto Conti, the minister of health. With a more open society and a longer experience with democracy, more women may have the chance to make some changes for the better. Paraguay has in place a legal framework that guarantees the protection of women's human rights. However, the laws are weak and often ineffective, so discrimination against women still persists in many areas. Some of the more pressing issues include a high maternal mortality rate, violence against women, low levels of political participation, and unemployment.

In 2017, Paraguay passed a law protecting women from violence and making provisions for legal assistance and shelters for survivors. As of 2018, regulations and an implementation plan were being developed.

accompanied by an expensive, elaborate reception. Consensual marriage is where the couple simply agrees to be married.

There is little difference in the status of the children of these various marriages, as long as the parents stay together and the father gives the child his last name. The only time a consensual union works to the child's disadvantage is if the father's family refuses to allow the child to use the family name or share in family inheritance at the death of the father. In this case, the child is treated almost as if he or she were illegitimate.

Often, men and women remain married to one another despite hardships. Sometimes even dangerous relationships result in people remaining together.

In Paraguay, there has been an increase in cases of domestic violence in the twenty-first century. In December 2017, Paraguay passed a new law to protect women against violence and provide assistance to survivors of domestic violence. There were nearly 13,500 reported cases of domestic violence in Paraguay that year, the highest number on record.

GENDER INEQUALITY

Women in the workplace earn substantially less than men do, despite equal or greater education. Women

A young Paraguayan woman teaches students at an agricultural school in Itapúa.

with six years of education or less earn only half of men's salaries in equivalent jobs, while women having seven to thirteen years of education earn only 71 percent of men's salaries for the same positions. Women outnumber men in professional and technical occupations, as well as in the workforce as a whole, but few women occupy the nation's administration and management jobs and other higher-level occupations.

The traditional role of the rural housewife is to raise children and tend the home. It is hard work, but rural women are the true backbone of the country. Not only are they expected to maintain the home, but they also do much of the field labor: haul water, collect firewood, plant crops, weed crops, harvest crops, and gather wild fruit. Men do the heavy labor: clear the land, plow it, and plant manioc.

When and if women speak up about their rights, they are considered egotistical and told they are not behaving in a feminine manner. This division of labor between the sexes and all the inequalities it embodies goes back to the first European-Guaraní marriages, where the men often treated women as only subhuman.

Despite difficulties, more women are advancing in the workforce. Rocío Casco is one of the few female lawmakers in the country. She has been pushing for acknowledgement of women's and gender rights in Paraguay. For example, she introduced the bill concerning women's rights in domestic violence incidents in 2016. Another woman making her mark in Paraguay is Sonia Brucke. She

"I would like especially to mention you, the women, wives and mothers of Paraguay, who at great cost and sacrifice were able to lift up a country defeated, devastated and laid low by an abominable war."

–Pope Francis

started the Ministry of Women, a government organization that works to advocate for women's rights around the country. She is also the director of a legislative commission on equality, gender, and development in Paraguay.

MILESTONES

Important milestones in a Paraguayan's life are baptism, marriage, and death. All three occasions are times when the family gathers to reassert its connections. For those who believe in Christianity, baptism is considered essential, since this is when the child is first brought to God's attention and blessed in church. Other rites prescribed by the Catholic Church include First Holy Communion and Confirmation, when children become more fully integrated into the church. Many poor people forego such rites, having little access to church or money to pay for celebrations. Weddings tend to be church affairs too. Men and women dress simply, and get their union recognized through an officiate, such as a priest. Often, these events are small. A couple saves for their ceremony and reception themselves. They also enjoy practical gifts, such as materials that will help them in their life together—money, silverware, and bedsheets are typical examples. Marriage, as we have seen, can be more or less formal depending on financial circumstances. Funerals are similar to those in North America, except that instead of displaying the dead person in a funeral home, rural families do everything at home. Traditionally the dead person lies in state for nine days. On the ninth night, everyone gathers to tell stories and console each other before the burial. Everyone close to the deceased is expected to wear black.

SCHOOLS

The history of education in Paraguay is one of unequal access and very slow expansion to meet the needs of the people. During the colonial period, only the very rich sent their children to school. From independence until the War of the Triple Alliance ended, educational facilities showed little progress. The single secondary school in existence closed in 1822. The only dictator of the period to do anything about education was Carlos Antonio López, who opened

four hundred elementary schools. By 1870, 14 percent of the population was literate. After the war, more effort went into improving education. The first public secondary school was opened in 1877, and the National University in Asunción was founded in 1889. In 1896, the first teacher training college opened its doors. There continued to be slow progress up to World War II, with more secondary schools and technical training schools opening. The real boost to education followed World War II—elementary school registration increased steadily then, but there was still a high degree of illiteracy in the countryside.

In the twenty-first century, steps have been taken to make education more accessible. Spending on education has increased, reaching 4.5 percent of GDP in 2016, up from 1.7 percent in 1989. Much of the increased funding has raised teacher salaries and updated curricula. There are several systems of education as well. Primary school goes from grades one to six; secondary school

This is a rural Paraguayan school in a Guaraní community.

goes from grades seven to twelve. There are two divisions within secondary school: lower and upper. Lower secondary spans grades seven to nine, and upper secondary stretches from ten to twelve. Following secondary school, there is the option for trade schools or university.

Students are required to attend school from ages six to twelve. Public education is free to all. The school year typically runs from February to December. While the majority of students attend school and get an education, as of 2014 about 17 percent of education-age students were not enrolled in school. The reasons for this are numerous. Perhaps schools are understaffed. If one teacher is expected to teach many students or multiple grades, students get little attention and learn more slowly. Poverty also plays a big role in school dropout rates and failures. Poor families often move around in response to demand for labor. Therefore, they miss out on valuable learning periods.

Children with no fixed address do not get registered for school. Poorer health care in the countryside means greater absenteeism due to illness. Finally, language is an issue. Rural children speak Guaraní at home, but classroom instruction is in Spanish. Many children have a difficult time adjusting to a second language.

As part of the educational reforms of the 1990s, the government created ten new universities, but the entire system is regarded as poor in quality. Most of the top universities in the country are based in Asunción. Universidad Nacional de Asunción and Universidad Autónoma de Asunción are the best ranked as of 2018.

In 2003, Paraguay's national military academy admitted female cadets for the first time, opening another door for women pursuing education. In 2015, Paraguay had an estimated literacy rate of 95 percent, with very little differential between men and women (95.8 percent and 94.3 percent, respectively). Illiteracy rates exceed the national average in rural areas.

HEALTH CARE

In terms of major indicators, health in Paraguay ranks near the median among South American countries. In 2017, Paraguay had an infant mortality rate of 18.7 deaths per 1,000 births, ranking it behind Argentina, Colombia, Brazil,

TRADITIONAL HEALERS

Indigenous tribes have encountered difficulties accessing immediate, professional, modern health care. This is largely due to the fact that most hospitals and clinics are based in cities, whereas indigenous communities live in remote or rural areas. As a result, the indigenous people have looked to traditional healers, called shamans, for their health practices.

A shaman is a person believed to have special powers. People believe that a person falls ill when a foreign object invades the body. The shaman goes into a trance in order to visualize the object and its location and then uses special chants and medicines to remove it.

Traditionally, shamans were very powerful in indigenous societies. In addition to their gift of healing the sick, they were also believed to be able to tell the future and guide the decisions of the group. People do not choose to be shamans. They are "chosen" by the spirits by being given special "sight" into the supernatural world. By going into trances, they communicate with unseen forces and use these to help them diagnose disease or predict the future.

Western medicine has long ridiculed these types of medical practitioners, and it is true that they cannot solve problems such as malnutrition with their magic. However, studies have shown that some kinds of illnesses do respond to this type of treatment, as long as the sick person really believes that he or she is being cured. Some people believe that the human mind can heal the body if it is convinced that it is being healed.

and Uruguay, but ahead of Bolivia. The health of Paraguayans living outside urban areas is generally worse than the health of those residing in cities. Many preventable diseases run rampant in rural regions. Parasitic and respiratory diseases, which could be controlled with proper medical treatment, drag down Paraguay's overall health. In general, malnutrition, lack of proper health care, and poor sanitation are the root of many health problems in Paraguay. Likewise,

Homes made from adobe can still be seen today.

viruses such as the Zika virus have caused health issues among residents in the twenty-first century.

Health care funding from the national government increased gradually throughout the 1980s and 1990s. Spending on health care rose to 1.7 percent of GDP in 2000, nearly triple the 0.6 percent of GDP spent in 1989. During the past decade, improvement in health care has increased. In 2014, spending on health care was 9.8 percent of GDP, up from 7.1 percent in 2009. Most of the money spent on private health care is on a fee-for-service basis, effectively preventing the poor population from seeing private doctors. According to 2018 estimates, Paraguay has about 129 physicians per 100,000 people.

HOMES

Many of the houses in Paraguay are considered inadequate. The National Department of Housing estimates that at least 1.1 million homes are needed in

Paraguay. According to the Inter-American Development Bank, about 43 percent of families live in inadequate houses. Housing problems include overcrowding, bad water and electrical systems, and poor sanitation.

In Paraguay, many of the wealthy live in mansions that would amaze many people for their size and luxury. At the other end of the spectrum, many poor Paraguayans live in inadequate housing. This is true in the cities and countryside alike.

Housing is directly related to the country's health problems, since many killer diseases in Paraguay can be prevented by the provision of clean water and sanitation. Diarrhea, which kills many babies and children around the world, is caused by the use of contaminated water and food. Small children's bodies react to the bacteria by trying to eliminate them through the bowels. This causes dehydration, since much of the body's fluids are lost. When more water is given, if that is contaminated, too, the problem worsens and eventually the child dies of dehydration and loss of essential salts. Simply by providing clean water, many infant deaths can be prevented. Paraguay must remedy its housing situation in order to improve the country's health.

Fortunately, in recent years housing quality and access to clean water has improved. Habitat for Humanity Paraguay has been working to improve housing conditions since 1998, building new homes as well as making repairs and improvements to existing homes. In September 2018, a new National Housing and Habitat Policy was passed in Paraguay, with the intent of changing the way the country addresses housing problems. It is hoped that in time, this policy will decrease the housing deficit.

INTERNET LINKS

https://www.habitat.org/where-we-build/paraguay
This website explores Habitat for Humanity in Paraguay.

http://www.visitparaguay.net
This website contains information about life and culture in Paraguay.

RELIGION

This is a Catholic church in the city of Encarnación.

8

RELIGION IS IMPORTANT TO MANY Paraguayans. Although people are allowed to practice any religion, many belong to the Christian faith. Religious holidays and some holy days are often national days off.

The Guaraní believe
that every person
has two souls.

RELIGIOUS BELIEFS

For the most part, religion in Paraguay is a mesh between Guaraní and Spanish beliefs. Today the majority of Paraguayans are Roman Catholic. Not all who identify as Catholic practice the religion, though.

Other Christian groups include Protestants, Evangelical Christians, Mennonites, and Jehovah's Witnesses. There are also several indigenous religions in Paraguay, as well as Buddhist, Jewish, and Muslim communities. Regardless of faith, for many, religion is a way to connect with others and celebrate what they believe.

BELIEFS OF THE GUARANÍ

Guaraní believe in the existence of gods. They call the creator of their world Ñanderuvuçú, a god living in a dark region, separated from his wife, Ñandeçy, who is known as Our Mother. Tupa, Ñandeçy's son, is the thunder god, and Yahira is the god who controls death and vengeance. Like the believers of many other religions, Guaraní pray to their gods for protection and help.

Guaraní also believe that every human has two souls: a "god-soul" that endows a person with peace, gentleness, and a craving for vegetables, and an "animal soul" that decides character. A person with a butterfly soul is patient and friendly, while one with a jaguar soul is cruel and brutal. Guaraní believe dreams are the souls' experiences, so they place importance on the interpretation of dreams. When a person dies, the souls are supposed to depart and go their separate ways. If the Guaraní believe the souls are hovering near the deceased, thus endangering the living, they call in shamans to perform rituals that send the souls on their way.

Finally, Guaraní believe that natural things such as plants and animals possess a spirit, which can be good or evil depending on how it is treated. As forest-dwellers, Guaraní believe that the natural world must be treated with respect in order not to offend these spirits.

THE MAJORITY RELIGION

About 90 percent of the population is Roman Catholic, but the Catholic Church has not played as large a role in Paraguayan life and politics as it has in other Latin American countries. Despite an overwhelming Catholic majority, the 1992 constitution does not recognize an official state religion and guarantees freedom of religion. The constitution also emphasizes Paraguay's independence from the Catholic Church.

In the colonial period, Paraguay was the site of the first diocese created in South America (1547). Travel was so difficult that only half of the first forty bishops assigned to Asunción arrived. The Catholic Church in Paraguay was often leaderless. After independence, Francia confiscated church lands and closed religious schools. Successive dictators were not as antireligious, but it was not until 1894 that another bishop was assigned to Paraguay. People remained Catholic, but participation in church activities declined because of the lack of priests. From the turn of the twentieth century until Stroessner's regime, the Catholic Church stayed out of politics.

After a meeting of Latin American Catholic bishops in Medellín, Colombia, in 1968, the Catholic Church became more involved in politics, pledging itself to help the poor and stand up for the rights of the abused. From 1968, priests worked with labor unions to help rural workers, organized Christian American Leagues to bring literacy and health services to the poor, and tried to get workers to organize themselves into unions to fight for their rights. Stroessner responded with repression, arresting or exiling many league leaders. In the 1970s, church-state relations worsened. The archbishop refused to sit on the Council of State, citing human rights abuse, and even excommunicated members of Stroessner's government

Weddings are an important rite of passage as well as an opportunity for a community gathering.

who were responsible for deaths and torture. Near the end of Stroessner's regime, the Catholic Church organized the National Dialogue—discussions among social and political leaders to criticize Stroessner, which he strongly resented. Things came to a head with the visit of Pope John Paul II in 1988. Throughout his stay, the pope talked about the need for a better human rights record and more freedom of speech and political participation. He gave his support to Catholic groups representing the poor and repressed. When Rodríguez took over in 1989, he promised to improve church-state relations. The Catholic Church's strong reputation among citizens for its work on their behalf gives it political weight.

The role of the church in everyday life is to provide a focus for community activities. Catholics in Paraguay celebrate important saints' days as a group and place importance on religious rites of passage, such as baptism, confirmation, marriage, and death, when people gather to celebrate the change in status of one of their members.

REDUCCIONES

Although the Catholic Church was generally not involved in the lives of Paraguayans until modern times, this was not true for Guaraní during the colonial period. A group of priests called Jesuits (from the Society of Jesus) started working with indigenous people in Brazil in 1607. They soon realized that European settlers were regularly rounding up thousands of Guaraní for slave labor on their farms. The Jesuits decided to remove the Guaraní from contact with Europeans. In 1609, they began to build Guaraní communities known as *reducciones* or missions; eventually there were more than thirty in eastern Paraguay, northeast Argentina, and southwest Brazil. These missions were to educate indigenous people in Catholicism, teach them basic skills and trades, and protect them from other Europeans.

More than 1,500 Jesuits from all over Europe dedicated their lives to *reducciones*. The work was hard and many people died of disease or exhaustion. Each *reducción* held two thousand to four thousand Guaraní and was self-sufficient in food and clothing. Residents also devoted part of each day to education and to learning Guaraní ways. The Jesuits were the first to try to record a Guaraní dictionary.

Many have argued that the Jesuits were too paternalistic, assuming the role of parents over their Guaraní "children." This is correct to some extent, but the *reducciones* were arguably better for the Guaraní than the *encomienda* system that gave Guaraní to individual settlers, and may have saved the lives of some eighty thousand Guaraní who otherwise could have been enslaved or killed by European settlers. As the *reducciones* flourished in the 1700s, European settlers became envious of their success and of the power of the Jesuits in Latin America. Back in Europe, people started agitating with the Spanish king to get rid of them. The Europeans wanted not only the land in the *reducciones*, but also the labor of the indigenous people there.

By 1767, they were successful; the Jesuits were forced to leave the *reducciones* and South America. Without the priests to lead and protect them, the Guaraní dispersed, and many were forced to work on European farms. Some wandered back into the forest, but many ended up in Asunción looking for work. This was a sad moment for the Guaraní. The *reducción* buildings fell into disrepair and were looted by settlers to build their own houses. Francia went so far as to destroy many *reducción* buildings, and Carlos Antonio López confiscated all remaining *reducción* lands.

RELIGIOUS MINORITIES

In the country's last national census, in 2002, 6.2 percent of the population of Paraguay was reported as Evangelical Christian, although those numbers

Although the reducciones *were left in ruins for a long time, archaeologists have spent years working in the rubble, restoring the most intact structures and learning how the Guaraní lived during this period. Two* reducción *sites, La Santísima Trinidad de Paraná and Jesús de Tavarangue, are the most complete and well known today. They have been UNESCO World Heritage sites since 1993.*

From the remains, we know that the church was the biggest and most central reducción *building on a mission. It dominated a central plaza or square. On either side of the church were the cemetery and the priests' residence. Also on the main square were the school, workshops, and the "big house" for orphans and widows. Guaraní families each had a small house or a segment of a long, subdivided house for their own use. There were common areas around these dwellings so that people could live and work together as they had been accustomed to doing in the forest.*

Behind the church was a garden. Land in the reducción *was commonly owned and worked. Every family contributed labor to mission activities, and no one owned the products of their own labor. This communal system is part of the reason that the missions were so successful. The Guaraní did not have a strong sense of private property, and they worked well as a group. The missions were so productive that they often sold extra food and manufactured items to other Europeans. The Jesuits forbade any other Europeans to live in the* reducciones, *thereby protecting the Guaraní from other European influence. They were even able to retain some of their beliefs and traditions. Many Guaraní became amazing craftspeople under the tutelage of the Jesuits.*

most likely have changed in the years since. Many belonging to Evangelical churches have spent time trying to convert the rural poor and especially poor indigenous people to their faith. Some criticize their involvement with indigenous groups, claiming that they have helped the government subdue and repress indigenous culture.

A Muslim man prays at the Alkhaulafa al-Rashdeen mosque in Ciudad del Este.

MENNONITES   The Mennonites are a Protestant sect founded in Europe in 1526. They believe in strict adherence to the scriptures and adult baptism, and are pacifists. Over the centuries, Mennonites have migrated to places that will let them live as they choose. At the turn of the twentieth century, Mennonites in Canada, Germany, and Russia were forced to move. Two destinations in Latin America at the time were very popular: Mexico and Paraguay.

Paraguay was attractive because it had lots of unused land in the Chaco, and the government promised to let the Mennonites live as they wanted. They did not have to do military service or pay taxes, but were responsible for their own German-language schools and local law enforcement. The first group came from Canada in 1927 and founded a settlement at Loma Plata. The second group, from Russia, founded Filadelfia in the 1930s. Finally, in 1947, a third group arrived who had been forced to serve in the German army during World War II. They settled at Neu-Halbstadt.

Although the government gave them guarantees that they could live however they chose, the Mennonites soon realized they had settled in an area that was by no means peaceful. The Chaco was disputed by Bolivians and Paraguayans during the Chaco War, and Chaco indigenous groups were not always happy to see the new settlers. Over time, a relationship developed between Mennonites and indigenous people: Those who wanted to convert to the Mennonite religion were welcome to settle alongside the Mennonites, though they had to maintain their own church. Non-Christian indigenous people—those who had not settled—worked as part-time laborers for the Mennonites.

JUDAISM   The Jewish community has around one thousand members who live mainly in Asunción. Asunción has three synagogues: Ashkenazi, Sephardi, and Chabad, and a Jewish museum as well.

ISLAM   There is a growing Muslim population representing about 0.1 percent of the population. Most of the Muslims are immigrants or descendants of immigrants from Syria and Lebanon. The community is concentrated in and around the capital, Asunción.

When two cultures coexist for a long time, elements of each are often combined to form a new blend. This process, called syncretism, is part of Paraguayan culture today. The blended culture shows many elements from both Guaraní heritage and Spanish influence. One area where this is obvious is in religion. The majority of Paraguayans are Roman Catholics now, but some of their beliefs still reflect Guaraní religious beliefs. For example, many rural people fear the evil spirits of Guaraní folklore. Here is the story of how some of these evil spirits were created:

A long time ago, an extraordinarily beautiful girl was born. The evil god Tau decided he wanted her and attacked her. Arasy, a female god, cursed him so that the girl's union with Tau produced seven evil and monstrous sons. One was a huge lizard with seven dog heads. The second was a serpent with a parrot's beak. The third was also a serpent but with horns and dangerous teeth. The fourth was a little man with golden hair who could make himself invisible. The fifth was a god who ate humans. The sixth attacked women and children. The seventh, Luisón, a wolf-man, was the god of the night and accompanied death. He liked to wander around cemeteries.

Some rural Paraguayans still fear these gods and demons and sometimes claim to hear them, especially Luisón, as they pass near bushes at night.

INTERNET LINKS

http://www.ancient-origins.net/myths-legends-americas/gods-creation-and-legendary-beasts-guarani-002937
This website contains information about the Guaraní creation story and gods.

http://whc.unesco.org/en/list/648
This is the UNESCO website containing information about the Jesuit missions in Paraguay.

LANGUAGE

AUDITÓRIO
Auditorio / Auditorium

ITAIPU
BINACIONAL

A sign at the Itaipú Dam directs visitors to the auditorium in three languages.

PARAGUAY IS A UNIQUE NATION WITH two distinct, nationally recognized languages. It is the only country in the Western Hemisphere to have most of its citizens speak an indigenous language rather than a European-influenced tongue. Many people who live in the country are bilingual. They use language and other modes, such as gestures, to communicate with others in everyday life.

9

Many Paraguayans believe that speaking the Guaraní language is what makes them distinctly Paraguayan.

A BILINGUAL NATION

There are two official languages in Paraguay: Spanish, as a result of years of colonialism, and Guaraní, an indigenous language that evolved from the southern dialect of the Tupí-Guaraní group. Which language is dominant depends on the region. Guaraní is most common in rural areas, and Spanish is spoken more in urban areas. Guaraní is spoken by most Paraguayans, and many rural people speak Spanish as a second language. The Guaraní language is a major part of Paraguay's national identity.

The two official languages are recognized in Paraguay's 1992 constitution. Spanish is used almost exclusively in government and business. More Paraguayans speak Guaraní than Spanish. Some 90 percent of the people in this bilingual country speak Guaraní, whereas only 75 percent speak Spanish. At least half of Paraguay's population can

Guaraní persisted
with enough vigor
to be made official
because the
Jesuits elected it
as the language
to preach Roman
Catholicism
to the Guaraní
and because
Paraguay's
dictators for a time
shut the country's
borders and
thereby protected
the local culture
and language.

speak both languages. All of Paraguay's presidents have been able to speak Guaraní, and many have used this to gain popularity.

Official policy on the value of Guaraní has changed over the years. After independence in 1811, the use of Guaraní in the classroom was banned. This did not change the national language because so few people went to school then. When Carlos Antonio López expanded education in rural areas, Spanish was the only language of instruction. His son, Francisco Solano López, used Guaraní as a symbol of nationalism—something that made Paraguayans distinct from Argentines and Uruguayans (two of Paraguay's three enemies in the War of the Triple Alliance). Guaraní was also very useful in hindering the enemies' understanding of Paraguayan communications during the War of the Triple Alliance.

When Paraguay lost the war, Guaraní was once again scorned by the new elite, who tried to copy the Argentines in matters of culture. Although Guaraní had no social status in the late nineteenth and early twentieth centuries, most rural people continued to speak it and were largely monolingual. Spanish was heard only among the wealthy of Asunción. During the Chaco War, Paraguayan generals realized that they could use Guaraní to prevent the Bolivians from understanding their orders. They forbade the use of Spanish on the battlefield, and when Paraguay won the war, the use of Guaraní became a matter of national pride.

Despite the abundant use and understanding of Guaraní, Spanish has traditionally been considered the language of educated people. In fact, the Guaraní word for "Spanish language" means "language of the masters." Knowledge of the Spanish language helps a person participate in business or politics. To get ahead in Paraguay and the rest of the world, one must speak Spanish well. Almost all newspapers in Paraguay are published in Spanish.

Many feel that Spanish is the language of superior people. At the same time, Guaraní is what makes them distinctly Paraguayan. In recent years, public use of Guaraní and pride in the language seems to have increased.

Today, Guaraní is a mandatory subject taught in all schools. However, not all people appreciate that. Some parents of students in school argue they want their children to learn languages other than Guaraní so that they might have more promising job prospects in the future. Moreover, the language has a formal and a colloquial version. Schools typically teach the formal, which does not seem much like the version spoken during sports matches or on the streets. This informal tongue is called *yopará* and combines Spanish and Guaraní words. There is no standardized written form of the language either, which has led to debates about how and which version should be taught. Without a standardized language, some people think Guaraní could move closer to extinction, as more people might be dissuaded from learning it and instead opt to use Spanish.

The government has been taking steps to embrace and elevate the Guaraní language. In 2017, more governmental department workers, so often using Spanish to communicate, were being taught Guaraní. Likewise, in court, people now have the option of having a trial in Spanish or in Guaraní. This is largely to do with a desire to uphold the 1992 constitution's pledge to bring the Guaraní language to the same level as Spanish. For so long, the language has suffered and been persecuted, despite everyone speaking it in the privacy of their homes. In the twenty-first century, more is being done to include it as truly a national tongue.

DIFFERENT VARIETIES OF LANGUAGE

The majority of Paraguayans speak a type of Spanish that is influenced by Guaraní. People who use this language include Guaraní words and Spanish words together in one sentence with a grammatical form that suits the words they have chosen. This total mixture of languages is called *guarañol* (gwar-ahn-YOHL), and some experts have suggested that it is a third, separate language.

In between fluent speakers of Spanish and *guarañol* speakers are "bilinguals"—those capable of speaking both languages well. They often switch to another language in mid-sentence but always use the correct grammar for whatever language they are speaking. This is called code-switching and is an interesting habit among bilingual populations.

When one language is more valued (Spanish, in this example) than the other, there are distinct patterns in code-switching. The valued language is used in formal circumstances, such as talking to one's boss or discussing intellectual subjects, while the other language is used among friends in social situations,

Tupí-Guaraní is the name of the linguistic family that includes Guaraní. Before the Europeans arrived, Guaraní people had expanded their territory to include a large segment of the coast of modern Brazil, and from the Atlantic Ocean all the way inland to the Paraná, Uruguay, and Paraguay Rivers. Numerically, they formed the biggest indigenous group in this region. For this reason, Guaraní was the first, and sometimes the only, native language used by conquistadors and Spanish priests trying to convert the indigenous people to Christianity. The Jesuits created the first dictionaries of Guaraní, and Guaraní is still spoken widely today.

These are a few few words and phrases in Guaraní:

English	Guaraní	Pronunciation
I.	che	chay
you	nde	nday
we	ñande	NYAN-day
big	guazú	gwah-ZOO
small	mishí	mee-SHEE
How are you?	Mba'eichapa?	mbah ay-ee-CHAH-pah?

at home, or when joking. Sometimes people code-switch in mid-conversation. This is because they find it easier to express themselves on different topics in one or the other language. This happens especially when only one language is taught in school or published in books and newspapers (as is mostly the case in Paraguay). Thus, when people are talking about their everyday lives, they tend to use Guaraní, but when they want to talk about the news or academic subjects, they switch to Spanish.

Some Guaraní words that have become a permanent part of Paraguayan Spanish include *ñandú* (nyan-DOO, meaning "rhea"), *ñanduti* (meaning "Paraguayan lace"), and many other words for animals, plants, and weather patterns. A speaker of standard Spanish who listens to Paraguayans speak their version of Spanish could be quite confused. Likewise, Guaraní has picked up Spanish words and pronunciations over five centuries of contact between the two languages—it is no longer the Guaraní that was spoken when the Spaniards first arrived. Language is one of the most dynamic areas of Paraguayan culture.

MINORITY LANGUAGES

Due to the isolation of much of the countryside throughout most of the nation's history, other languages have survived in Paraguay. Aside from Guaraní, at least four other native languages are still spoken in the Chaco region. These languages have survived because their speakers have been left alone for most of the last five hundred years. During the twentieth century, these native groups were forced to have more contact with nonnative peoples. Now many of them are bilingual in at least one other language, often Guaraní.

Stroessner did not care much about the rights or culture of Paraguay's remaining indigenous peoples, and consequently they were under constant threat of cultural destruction. The democratic Paraguayan state that followed, beginning with Wasmosy, has made greater efforts to protect indigenous groups and thereby help preserve their languages.

Besides Spanish, other nonnative languages are spoken in Paraguay. The largest group, the German-speaking Mennonites, came to Paraguay in part because the government promised them that they could continue to speak their form of German. There are Mennonite schools that teach German in their settlements.

The Japanese have also retained the use of their language. At first they taught their children only Japanese, but more recently they decided to integrate more fully with Paraguayan society. Now children of Japanese descent learn in Spanish, while Japanese is taught as a second language.

In Paraguay's Mennonite communities, signs are in both Spanish (*top*) and German (*bottom*).

INTERNET LINKS

http://aboutworldlanguages.com/guarani
This website contains information about the history, structure, and grammar of the Guaraní language.

http://www.omniglot.com/writing/guarani.htm
This online encyclopedia of writing systems and languages features information about the Guaraní language, including its alphabet.

ARTS

Ñandutí lace in bright colors is displayed at an Asunción street market.

FOR MANY DECADES, PARAGUAYANS had limited avenues for expressing and enjoying fine arts. After gaining independence in 1811, dictator José Gaspar Rodríguez de Francia controlled the country. He not only closed the borders to prevent any contact with larger populations in Buenos Aires and around the world, but he also closed the schools. This had a detrimental effect on the arts.

10

Paraguayan arts suffered during the years of dictatorial rule and various wars, and only revived when democracy was restored.

SLOWLY RECOVERING

The arts did not begin to recover from this isolation until after the War of the Triple Alliance, although Francisco Solano López introduced theater to Paraguay during his reign. In the twentieth century, unstable and repressive governments muffled literary and artistic aspirations. Today, the government still provides very little funding to the arts, and some artists and musicians have left Paraguay to work in other countries. However, Asunción is home to many cultural institutions, including the Conservatory of Music, the National Academy of Fine Arts, and the Asunción Symphony Orchestra. Paraguay also has many museums and art galleries.

Art and literature in Paraguay reflect both Guaraní and Spanish traditions. Paraguay also has a vibrant and colorful tradition of folk art,

and many of its crafts rival any in the world for their beauty and distinctiveness. The most well-known is *ñandutí* lace, which combines sixteenth-century European lace-making techniques with Guaraní tradition.

LITERATURE

The first real wave of Paraguayan writers is known as the Generation of 1870 because they all started writing after the end of the War of the Triple Alliance. These men (there were no women) combined writing with politics, and the latter usually influenced the former.

One writer and art patron of this epoch was Juan Silvano Godoi. Another influential writer and politician of the era was Cecilio Báez, born in 1862 and a lawyer by profession. He wrote for newspapers and advocated democracy and free trade rules as the answer to Paraguay's continual political turmoil. He was responsible for the formal organization of the Liberal Party in 1887 and was instrumental in overthrowing the Colorados in 1904.

Like Báez, most other writers of this generation were Liberals, and many of them held important government positions or were quite powerful behind the scenes. Most of the books published in this period were histories of Paraguay or political commentaries on the future of Paraguay. They are characterized by their extreme patriotism and rather biased interpretations of history.

In the twentieth century, a new generation of writers emerged who were largely the product of the Chaco War. This war was very significant to Paraguayans, as it was to Bolivians. Many people were forced to think long and hard about their country's history and its future. In North America and Europe, a parallel can be drawn with World War I, since it was so traumatic for all people involved that it sparked a change in outlook.

These new writers tended to focus on fiction rather than history, but they were also drawn into politics, mostly by virtue of being exiled from the country by one or more regimes. Stroessner was particularly intolerant, so some of Paraguay's best twentieth-century writers lived most of their lives outside Paraguay. Augusto Roa Bastos is a good example. Another is Gabriel Casaccia, born in Asunción in 1907 and exiled to Argentina by 1935. All of his novels were published in Buenos Aires, and all deal with the hopelessness of

Augusto Roa Bastos was born in Paraguay in 1917 and raised by his uncle, a bishop, in the jungle. Like many members of his generation, he fought in the Chaco War and was permanently altered by his experiences of violence and brutality. He started writing as a young man and continued when he returned from the war, though he never completed his education. His first novel was never published, although it won a local literary prize.

He worked as a journalist for an Asunción paper and was sent to Europe to cover World War II. When he returned to Paraguay in 1945, he was exiled for political reasons and for some time lived in Buenos Aires. There he continued writing and became involved with the Argentine motion-picture industry. Some of his books have been made into films. In 1960, he published Son of Man, *a novel about the Chaco War that was later translated into English. The book is about one individual's struggle for freedom and how solidarity among people can spring from adversity. His most acclaimed novel,* I, the Supreme, *is about Paraguay's first dictator, Francia. It was first published in 1974 and translated into English in 1986.*

Following the downfall of the oppressive Stroessner regime in 1989, Roa Bastos returned to Paraguay at the request of its new leader, Andrés Rodríguez. Roa Bastos died of a heart attack on April 26, 2005, in Asunción.

the politically and morally corrupt society in Paraguay. He died in 1980, never having returned to his country.

The number of books published in Paraguay increased significantly in 1989, after the fall of Stroessner's regime. Poetry also gained more success, with the works of Roa Bastos and Josefina Plá being the most notable. Today, more people are getting involved in Paraguay's literary scene. Contemporary writers include Delfina Acosta, a writer, essayist, and poet who received literature awards in 2012 and 2016, and bilingual poet Susy Delgado, who publishes all of her poems in both Spanish and Guaraní and has won several awards.

FINE ART

Juan Silvano Godoi established the country's first museum featuring visual art, which he had to bring from abroad because there was nothing Paraguayan to display at the turn of the twentieth century. In the first three decades

JOSEFINA PLÁ

Paraguay's best-known and most influential female artist and cultural expert, Josefina Plá, was born in the Canary Islands in 1909 and came to Paraguay with her husband in 1927. Her earliest artistic endeavors were in poetry. Her first volume of poems, The Price of Dreams, *was published in 1934. During the Chaco War, she operated a radio station that presented dramas and comedies to the soldiers in the field. While organizing this, she brought together a variety of writers and actors who later formed the nucleus of Paraguay's postwar cultural scene.*

Her talents did not stop at poetry and organizing. She was also a sculptor whose work has been exhibited all over South America, and her murals and mosaics decorate important buildings in Asunción. Josefina Plá was also a historian. She wrote two books on the art of Paraguay: one on the art of the Jesuit missions and the other on plastic arts in Paraguay. She also wrote for the newspapers on a regular basis and was truly the grand dame of the Paraguayan art scene. Surrounded by the consideration and respect of artists and intellectuals from Paraguay, Spain, and all over the world, she died on January 20, 1999, in Asunción.

of the twentieth century, under Liberal rule, there was some interest in art exhibitions of local works. The first, held in 1918, attracted 209 paintings. Some artists of Paraguayan nationality who had been studying and exhibiting abroad returned to show their work for the first time. Two of these were Jaime Bestard and Juan Samudio.

The first woman painter to show her work in Asunción was Ofelia Echagüe Vera. She held her own exhibition in 1945 and met some success. She likewise dedicated herself to teaching others, having notable pupils such as Olga Blinder, Pedro di Lascio, and Aldo del Pino. In 1936, Jewish artist Wolf Bandurek immigrated to Paraguay from Germany, seeking refuge from the Nazis. His artwork is very dark and full of the terror of Nazi Germany. Josefina Plá was instrumental in bringing together people interested in promoting Paraguayan art at home and abroad.

As with all things artistic, visual art was not very productive during the Stroessner years. There were few artists in that era, and they had to contend with an indifferent state that was unwilling to fund projects or displays. Today, however, the Barro Museum in Asunción exhibits art from colonial to modern times, emphasizing modern and unconventional works of art.

This is the entrance to Asunción's Barro Museum.

GUARANÍ-BAROQUE   The two most famous Jesuit *reducciones* in Paraguay are La Santísima Trinidad de Paraná and Jesús de Tavarangue. Both are preserved as historic sites and are reminders of the miracles worked by the Jesuits and Guaraní people in the forests of eastern Paraguay. The main church and school buildings were all made of stone that was hand cut and carried to the site. Their architecture shows how creative the designers could be using simple tools and materials. In addition, church pulpits and arches are exquisitely carved with angels and other religious icons. In 1981, a collection of wooden statues was discovered in a burial tunnel at Santísima Trinidad. This is a veritable treasure, since most portable objects had long since been stolen and sold. The style of wood and stone carving is so distinct that art historians have given it its own name: Guaraní-Baroque.

The Guaraní were taught a Baroque style of carving popular in Europe in the seventeenth century. Guaraní carving is distinctive, reflecting both the Baroque style taught to them by the priests and their own vision of the natural world. Unlike the Classical style, which is simple and ordered, the Baroque is detailed and fluid. Carvings in this style often have complicated designs of leaves and vines twisting among angels or saints. The life-size statues of saints are said to capture emotions in their faces and are considered some of the finest religious art in the world.

THEATER

Asunción is Paraguay's center for the performing arts. There is a lively theater scene with productions in both Spanish and Guaraní. The first play in Guaraní, written by Julio Correa, was put on during the Chaco War in 1933. It was about the war and attracted crowds so large that the police had to be called in to manage them. This success derived in part from people's nationalism

Here, Paraguayan traditional dance is performed by the Municipal Folk Ballet of Asunción.

On October 26, 2013, Asunción was the location of the Guinness World Record for the largest harp ensemble, with 420 harp players from around the world participating.

during wartime and in part from the use of the Guaraní language. People spoke better Guaraní than Spanish then, and clearly they supported theater in their home language.

Today, Paraguay's theaters are in large cities, especially Anunción. Performances such as ballet, jazz, and plays happen every year. The Recycled Orchestra of Cateura has also gained international recognition.

MUSIC AND INSTRUMENTS

Two types of music are typically Paraguayan: the polka and the *guarania* (gwar-ah-NEE-ah). Polkas are adaptations of eastern European musical forms and dances. *Guaranias* are the love songs traditionally sung by a suitor to his beloved outside her window at night. This music uses a particularly Paraguayan ensemble of guitars and the Paraguayan harp, which looks much like the European harp of large symphonies but is made differently and sounds different. Paraguayan composer and harpist José Asunción Flores is credited with creating the *guarania* style, with its distinctive melancholy sound.

Many restaurants feature guitar and harp ensembles to entertain their guests. The Ballet Folklorico (Folkloric Ballet) holds frequent music and dance performances to preserve the tradition of the performing arts. Paraguayans frequently play music at social events and celebrations. Many learn to play either the Spanish-style guitar or the Paraguayan harp at a young age. Rock bands also began rising after the end of the dictatorship in 1989, and they remain popular in urban areas.

LA GALOPA   The *galopa* is a special dance performed by women only. It has gone out of fashion as a regular feature of rural life, but the Folkloric Ballet still performs it for tourists and Paraguayans. The dancers dress in typical nineteenth-century rural costumes and step to polka-like music while balancing bottles on their heads. A *galopera* (*galopa* dancer) may have as many as ten bottles balanced while dancing. The bottles are all attached to each other but not to her head, which makes balancing pretty tricky.

A MODERN MUSICIAN

One of the most well-known musicians of modern-day Paraguay is Victor Espinola. He was born in a small town. His family had a history of musical talent, which Espinola inherited. When he was seven, he received his first guitar. However, at age ten he became familiar with the Paraguayan harp. This instrument has shaped his musical career ever since. Today, Victor Espinola is an accomplished harp player and singer. His abilities have taken him around the world. He

has toured with famous musician Yanni for seven world tours, alongside his band the Forbidden Saints, as well as performed as a resident solo artist at Disney World in Florida from 2016 to 2018. He also performed with Italian tenor Alessandro Safina in his 2019 US tour. His styles embody a mix of flamenco, Brazilian, Middle Eastern, pop, and dance, and his talent has gained him followers around the globe.

The *galopa* originated as a dance for particular saints' days. Women would pray to saints for specific things; if they got them, they would dance at the festival to thank the saint. To make this more difficult, they would dance with a jug filled with water on their heads. When they finished the dance, they would offer the water to spectators, saying, "Thank you, Saint Blaise" or "Thank you, Holy Virgin" as each person drank from the jug. When they finished, they felt they had "paid" the saint back for whatever they had received. Sometimes women would dance just to show their faith to the saint.

TRADITIONAL CRAFTS

There is a wealth of handicrafts and folk art produced in Paraguay that can be classified by medium, starting with textiles. The most coveted textiles are the embroideries made in the cities of Guarambaré and Itauguá. Woven ponchos, known for their beauty and quality, are made by the Lengua, Maskoy, Chulupi, and Wichí ethnic groups from the Gran Chaco.

An artist creates *ñandutí* lace by hand.

TEXTILES   The most famous of Paraguay's handmade textiles is *ñandutí*, the "spider's web" cotton lace for which the town of Itauguá is famous. Itauguá holds a four-day Ñandutí Festival every year in early July. *Ahó poí* (ah-HOH POY) is a very fine handwoven cotton fabric first made when Francia closed the country's borders. Once denied access to imports, people had to manufacture their own cloth. The national dress is usually made with *ahó poí*. A rougher form of handmade cotton cloth is the *poyví* (poy-VEE). It is the material for ponchos, hammocks, and rugs rather than fine clothing. Sheep were introduced to the country in the seventeenth century, and since then there have been woolens produced by hand and now by machine.

LEATHER   With the introduction of cattle, leatherworking developed. The Jesuit missions were famous for their finely crafted leather, but such skills were lost with the death of craftsmen during the War of the Triple Alliance. Leatherworking was revived in the twentieth century, and Paraguayan products such as shoes and bags rival those from Argentina and Brazil.

WOODWORK   The most famous woodwork comes from the Chaco natives, who carve an aromatic wood called *palo santo* (PAH-loh SAHN-toh) into animal shapes and replicas of hunting weapons. In Luque, craftsmen make beautiful guitars and harps. Finally, the Guaraní statues made in *reducciones* have been revived as a folk art in Tobatí, where people use the same techniques and colors to create replicas of religious icons.

POTTERY   It is a thriving folk art and home industry. Most often, women are the potters, and their art reflects the Guaraní heritage. Most of today's ceramic ware is produced as art rather than for utility. A typical theme is the female figure in a variety of poses. Not so long ago, most houses had to collect water or have it delivered, and the water was stored in large jars. Modern potters are still making fanciful and beautiful jars as collector's pieces.

POTTER'S WORK

Pottery and ceramics have taken prominence in Paraguay's art scene in the twentieth and twenty-first centuries. One of the most accomplished potters was Rosa Brítez. Born in 1941, Brítez held exhibitions in numerous countries beginning in 1970 to display her pottery pieces representing Paraguayan culture. She was known for her distinctive use of black clay. Brítez passed away in December 2017, but her pottery lives on as her legacy.

BASKETRY   Guaraní craftswomen taught their children how to work with the fibers of plants such as the coconut palm and jungle vines. It is still a viable cottage industry for women.

JEWELRY   Last but not least is metalwork. Paraguay's jewelers are famous for gold and silver filigree work. Designs are made from wire twisted into complicated swirls and patterns and then formed into shapes either for use as jewelry or in home decoration. Filigree can also be wrapped around another material such as wood, horn, or glass to decorate containers such as glasses and sugar bowls.

INTERNET LINKS

http://oac.cdlib.org/findaid/ark:/13030/kt4779s0t4
Collection guide for the Juan Silvano Godoi Collection at the University of California library.

https://www.lonelyplanet.com/paraguay/asuncion/attractions/ museo-del-barro/a/poi-sig/436806/363375
This website briefly discusses details of the Barro Museum in Asunción.

https://www.poetrysoup.com/famous/poems/short/josefina_pla
This website features the poems of Josefina Plá.

LEISURE

Paraguayans cheer on their country's team at a 2017 soccer game in France. Soccer, or football, is a popular pastime in Paraguay.

11

P ARAGUAYANS HAVE A REPUTATION for being both hard-working and community-driven people. Outside of the cities, life moves at a slower pace. Most leisure time is family time, since family is so important to most Paraguayans. Poverty and location often affect the choice of activity. For example, Paraguayans enjoy swimming as a pastime, but this pleasure is more accessible to rural people living near rivers than the urban poor. Art and music are popular hobbies among those who can afford the necessary instruments and supplies.

ATHLETIC ACTIVITIES

The most popular sport in Paraguay is soccer, or football as it is called in many parts of the world, including Paraguay. This game became popular with schoolboys in England in the mid-1800s. Its simplicity and affordability soon made it popular with the working class. The game began to spread around the world in the late 1800s. It became popular in Latin America near the turn of the twentieth century and is now the sport of choice for the vast majority of people in South America.

Paraguay's first Olympic appearance was in 1968 in Mexico City. They have only ever won one medal at the Olympics—the silver in men's soccer in 2004. They lost 1–0 to Argentina in the final in Athens.

The popular Cerro Porteño soccer team poses before a game in 2018.

Soccer's widespread appeal is due to the fact that no special equipment is needed. Any ball of approximately the right size and weight will work, and it can be made out of locally available materials. Any piece of relatively flat land is the only other thing required, plus enthusiastic players, of course! Street soccer games can be seen throughout Paraguay. Children in poor rural areas often play in a dirt field, and more well-off neighborhoods have community soccer fields.

Paraguay's national men's soccer team remains popular in the country today. They last qualified in the World Cup in 2010, reaching the quarterfinals, and were runners-up in the 2011 Copa América, losing 3—0 to Uruguay. They fell just short of the quarterfinals in 2016, losing 1—0 to the United States. Smaller, local teams have also popped up around the country. People attend games, in stadiums as well as around the world, to cheer on their favorite players.

Paraguay has amateur teams as well as professional teams that compete in international soccer matches. The headquarters of the South American Football Confederation (Conmebol) is located in Luque, outside of Asunción. The largest stadium in Paraguay is in Asunción, and residents enjoy attending games or watching them on television. The most popular professional soccer teams are Olimpia and Cerro Porteño, which are rivals.

Other sports, mostly preferred by the wealthy, include golf, basketball, and horseracing. Basketball was introduced to South America in the 1890s, and it has gained popularity in the years since. Today, there are both men's and women's teams playing throughout Paraguay. Golf is one of the world's more expensive sports. Equipment is complicated and pricey, as are golf club memberships.

OTHER FORMS OF LEISURE

The Trans-Chaco Rally, a three-day driving competition, has been held annually along the dirt roads of the massive Trans-Chaco Highway since 1970. Thousands of people travel to the Chaco to watch the race.

Among Paraguayans who can afford it, going to the movies and watching television are popular. The film industry in Paraguay is small compared to those of neighboring Argentina and Brazil, and it has suffered from lack of funds, equipment, and public interest, as well as the repressive Alfredo Stroessner

A PARAGUAY VACATION

Paraguay has a small tourism industry, as it is not a very popular travel destination compared to other South American countries. However, since 2004, the number of people visiting Paraguay has been on the rise and reached a record high in 2015, at over 1.5 million. That is nearly double the number of visitors of the previous year. Most tourists come during major festivals such as Carnival, but others prefer bird-watching and leisure activities like hiking or boating.

Most visitors come from neighboring countries. For some, the attraction is cheaper shopping. Paraguay also has well-preserved national parks that attract wealthy tourists interested in ecotourism, a phenomenon that has become popular around the world wherever there are natural environments. This type of tourism aims to let people enjoy nature without disturbing it. Bird-watching is popular, as Paraguay has over seven hundred bird species. Tourists can also enjoy hikes in the rain forest and riverboat trips.

Besides natural wonders, Paraguay also offers visitors a taste of a different culture. For other Latin Americans, Paraguay is considered exotic because of its blend of Guaraní and Spanish cultures. One of the national cultural treasures is the collection of Jesuit reducciones found in the eastern region; the government has declared them protected sites and is trying to raise money to restore them properly to attract tourists.

government of 1954 to 1989. Many English films are screened with Spanish subtitles. Only large population centers have theaters. Some of Paraguay's rural areas are very remote. While even in rural areas 96 percent of the population had electricity as of 2013, that still leaves some one hundred thousand people without access. Also, only an estimated 51.3 percent of Paraguayans had internet access as of 2016. For the rest, leisure usually means passing the time with neighbors rather than hovering over TV screens or cell phones and computers.

The wealthy enjoy tourism in their own country. They make trips to the national parks or to less settled areas to fish or hunt. Fishing is particularly good in Paraguay and attracts fishing enthusiasts from abroad.

Throughout the year, everyone celebrates various festivals, the extent of their participation being guided by their means. In between, family rituals provide diversion. A baptism or marriage, for example, is a social event where neighbors help out and enjoy the festivities.

A group of Paraguayan women and children socialize together outside of a house in Asunción.

Some Guaraní games have survived in the countryside. One game is similar to badminton, except that no racket or net is used. The shuttlecock is made from corn leaves, and the object of the game is to hit it back and forth using the hands, without letting it fall to the ground.

FOLKTALES

For those who cannot afford organized leisure activities, there is always the age-old entertainment provided by storytelling. Before television and radio, and even before the printing press made books widely available, there was storytelling. Sitting around listening to the myths and legends of their culture was one way people learned their history and their religion. It functioned to bring the group together in a social setting and was—and is—a free form of entertainment.

Related to storytelling is the *guarania*, or love song, sung by a man to the woman he wishes to court. The man composes his own song to demonstrate the depth of his affection. Some *guaranias* have become popular, and people will also entertain themselves by singing and dancing to *guaranias* as a group.

STORIES OF THE MACÁ

Many indigenous stories, such as the stories of the Macá ethnic group, try to explain origins or relationships. In these mythical stories, animals may behave like people. Here is one example:

Once a man lived alone with his son near a lagoon. All the women of their village collected water from a lagoon. The man told the boy to go to the path leading to the lagoon and wait for the women to pass. He was to call each woman "Mother" until one of them accepted him as her son. He did this and all the women ignored him except the last one. She took him home with her and raised him. He was given a bow and arrows when he was older and became a very skilled hunter. One day he was hunting in the forest and he lost an arrow. When he found it, it was stuck in a plant. When he pulled the arrow out, a big dorado fish jumped out of the hole. He brought the fish home to his mother and every day returned to the special plant, for fish. A fox had been watching him secretly, and when the boy left one day, the fox started pulling out fish to eat. When he came to the biggest dorado of them all, it proved to be the master fish who ordered all the other fish to jump out of the plant bringing lots of water with them. The water carried the fish and fox into the rivers, and the fox had to turn into a gourd so he could float. That is how the fish got into the rivers.

INTERNET LINKS

https://www.lonelyplanet.com/paraguay/events/transchaco-rally/a/poi-fes/1279336/363374
This website contains information about the Trans-Chaco Rally.

https://us.soccerway.com/teams/paraguay/paraguay/1630
This website discusses statistics for the Paraguayan national soccer team.

FESTIVALS

Bullfights are a traditional part of the Festival of Saint Blaise, the patron saint of Paraguay, as well as of other festival days. The bull is not killed during the fight.

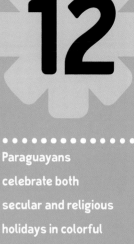

THE CATHOLIC INFLUENCE ON Paraguayan culture left by the Spanish can be seen strongly in many of the country's traditional holidays, which are religious in nature and based around the Catholic religion and saints. However, the unique Paraguayan culture has put its own spin on the festivals.

The period from February to July is the festival season in Paraguay. A large number of tourists visit the country during this time in order to witness the colorful festivities, particularly for Carnival. Paraguay holds a multi-day Carnival celebration right before the beginning of the Catholic tradition of Lent. Carnival is similar to the Mardi Gras festivals held in other countries, featuring parades and other festivities. It is the largest festival in Paraguay. Celebrations are held in many cities, but the largest is in the city of Encarnación.

EPIPHANY

In the Catholic calendar, Epiphany (January 6) is the day the Magi, or Three Kings, visited the baby Jesus and brought him gifts. Much of the religious significance of this day has faded in Paraguay. Just like Christmas in North America, Epiphany has become more secular.

In rural areas especially, people stage horse races and other games on horseback. They also have archery contests, and prizes are awarded to those possessing great skill with a bow and arrow. There may also be

This procession of people wearing masks and feathers celebrates Saint Francisco Solano, the patron saint of indigenous people.

a competition to see who can climb a greased pole the fastest. This is hilarious for spectators and extremely difficult for contestants.

Tobatí, a small town east of Asunción, holds a religious procession accompanied by men in extravagant masks. They make the masks themselves in the form of animals or humans, or a combination of the two. There are certain rules connected to this procession: they never use a mask more than once, and they remain anonymous while wearing it. The men cover even their hands so no one can guess the identity of the person behind each mask. Self-preservation is the reason for this secrecy. The masked entertainers tell jokes and tease people using false voices, offending many people with their antics. They accompany the religious procession but do not enter the church.

CELEBRATION OF THE PATRON SAINT

For Catholics, Saint Blaise is the patron saint of Paraguay and the saint of throats and throat afflictions. According to legend, Saint Blaise was being led to his execution in 316 CE when he cured a child suffering from a sore throat. Since then, Catholic sufferers of throat ailments have prayed to him.

Another story explains why he is the patron saint of Paraguay. In the early Spanish occupation of the place that would become Asunción, a fort was built to repel attacks from hostile indigenous people. On February 3, 1539, an apparition of a man in white on one of the fort's towers frightened away the attackers. Catholics believed that Saint Blaise appeared to rescue the Spaniards and proclaimed him the protector of Paraguay.

On February 3, processions are held in towns and in the countryside. The favorite attraction is a bullfight. The bull is decorated with paper streamers and flowers, and money is tied to its tail. The bullfighters do not try to kill the bull; they just try to get the money off the bull's tail without getting hurt, miming bullfighting techniques to entertain the crowds.

The city of Ciudad del Este holds the largest celebrations of this festival on Saint Blaise Day, holding events for up to a week leading up to it.

The Ñandutí Festival, centered around the traditional lace of the same name, is held in the city of Itauguá every July, showing off the region's crafts and cultural arts.

EASTER FESTIVITIES

This Christian holiday commemorates Jesus Christ's crucifixion on Good Friday and resurrection on Easter Sunday. Like most largely Catholic countries, Paraguay celebrates Easter not just on two days, but for a whole week. During this time there are religious processions through the streets, and Christians attend Mass, or service, regularly. People do not work or go to school during Easter week.

In Paraguay, on the Saturday before Easter, people put on plays and processions about Judas, Christ's disciple who betrayed him to the Romans with a kiss. They build life-size effigies, or replicas, of Judas and parade them through the streets. Then they stage a play in which "Judas" is tried and convicted for his crime of betrayal and a Judas effigy is hung or set on fire.

SAINTS JOHN AND PETER

June 24 and 29 are dedicated to Saint John the Baptist and Saint Peter, respectively. Saint John's Day has long been associated with bonfires in Europe. When the Catholic Church tried to replace pre-Catholic midsummer celebrations with this religious observance, early beliefs in natural elements such as fire were incorporated. The Festival of Saint John is celebrated with traditional games, one of which involves walking on hot coals. On June 24 in Paraguay, celebrations for Catholics begin with a special Mass in church.

The main spectacle of the festivities is the *toro candil*, or candle bull. This is actually a man dressed as a bull with kerosene-soaked rags attached to a tail and horns. The bull chases people playing music and taunting him. At night this is quite a sight as the horns and tail are on fire. At some point, another character enters the arena: a child dressed as a rhea, or ostrich-like bird, with a long stick for a neck and leaves for feathers. The child will also torment the bull by poking him from behind with the stick. A third character in this play is the *cheolo* (chay-OH-loh), a man who comes out of the crowd to challenge the bull. When all eyes are on the action, other men will charge into the crowds and start "kidnapping" women and girls. As they run off with the women, the remaining men will try to stop them. Young men in particular will try to bring

PARAGUAYAN FESTIVALS AND HOLIDAYS

January 1. . . . .New Year's Day

January 6. . . . .Epiphany, Day of the Kings

February 3 . . . .Saint Blaise Day, patron saint of Paraguay

February . . . . .Carnival (not as big as in other Latin countries such as Brazil and Uruguay)

March 1 . . . . .Heroes' Day

March/April . . .Holy Week, Easter

May 1. . . . . . .International Worker's Day or May Day

May 15 . . . . . .Independence Day

June 12 . . . . . .Chaco Peace Day

June 24 . . . . . .Festival of Saint John

June 29 . . . . . .Festival of Saint Peter

August 15 . . . .Founding of Asunción

August 25 . . . .Constitution Day

September 29. . Victory Day

October 12 . . . .Day of Race or Columbus Day (most other South American countries have changed this to Day of Indigenous Resistance, Decolonization Day, or similar names)

December 8 . . .Day of the Virgin of Caacupé

December 25. . .Christmas

back young women to their parents to show their masculinity. This play is so much fun for participants that they use Saint Peter's Day, five days later, to do it all over again!

Saint John's Day is also associated with superstitions. For example, some rural women believe they must cut their hair on this day or it will stop growing the rest of the year. Young women wanting to know who they will marry write the names of potential suitors on separate pieces of paper. They fold the pieces tightly and scatter them in the open, leaving them overnight. When they awake, the paper that has unfolded the most overnight reveals the name of their intended groom. A darker superstition says that anyone who looks in a mirror in the middle of the night of June 24 and does not see his or her reflection will die the following year.

FEAST OF THE IMMACULATE CONCEPTION

In the Catholic calendar, December 8 is the Feast of Immaculate Conception, or the day the Virgin Mary is believed to have conceived Jesus without sin. The image of the Virgin at Caacupé is thought by some Catholics to have miraculous powers. The image was discovered by a Franciscan monk many years ago. According to legend, the Virgin of Caacupé saved a converted Guaraní from a band of Mbayáes who were hostile to the Christian faith. To show his gratitude, he carved an image of the Lady of Caacupé out of a large yerba maté plant.

This is the most important religious festival in Paraguay. Thousands of people will make a pilgrimage to Caacupé for the special Mass and the celebrations which follow. Many Christians who come suffer afflictions or carry sick relatives in the hope that the image of the Virgin will heal them. On this day, Caacupé is converted into a town of festivities and attractions. Some Paraguayans bemoan the commercialism, saying they want it to be a purely religious celebration. Whenever lots of people gather, it seems that even more are attracted in order to sell things.

During the 1960s, the Paraguayan Catholic Church made this day a political tool against Stroessner's dictatorship. The Mass was used to criticize

The large number of German immigrants to Paraguay has led to the city of Asunción holding an Oktoberfest celebration each September, modeled after the German festival.

The image of the Virgin of Caacupé sits in the Basilica of Caacupé, near Asunción. It is an important destination for pilgrims each year.

Stroessner's abuse of human rights, and in 1969 the religious procession of the Virgin through the town was suspended as a protest against the regime. The suspension of the most cherished religious day of the year had some effect on Stroessner's popularity.

PATRIOTIC CELEBRATIONS

Paraguayans are very patriotic and celebrate many historic days. All of these days are usually observed as national holidays, though not all of them are legally designated as such. Independence is celebrated on May 15 to commemorate the bloodless coup that gave Paraguay its freedom from Spanish and Argentine control in 1811. This day is one of elaborate street parades in the capital city. People wear the national dress or the national colors of red, white, and blue. The national anthem is sung in the main square, and there are fireworks at night. Paraguayans also celebrate Independence Day with barbecues, soccer games, music, and drinks. Outside Asunción, many other towns and cities hold their own parades.

Constitution Day (August 25) celebrates the signing of the 1967 document. August 15 commemorates the founding of Asunción. Two days are dedicated to remembering the Chaco War: June 12 and September 29. The first celebrates the signing of the peace treaty between Paraguay and Bolivia, while the second commemorates the Battle of Boquerón, when the Paraguayans scored an important victory. Heroes' Day is for those who died in the War of the Triple Alliance: March 1 was when the final battle at Cerro Corá was lost and Francisco Solano López was killed. Other holidays that are observed in Paraguay include New Year's Day, Christmas, International Labor Day or May Day (observed since 1906), and Day of Race (October 12), which has historically commemorated the arrival in America of Christopher Columbus and indigenous peoples' contribution to Latin America. Today, many Latin American countries have done away with the name Day of Race in favor of acknowledging the suffering of indigenous people under Spanish colonization. This day is now known as Decolonization Day in Bolivia, Day of Indigenous Resistance in Venezuela and Nicaragua, and Day of Respect for Cultural Diversity in Argentina.

The national anthem of Paraguay was adopted in 1846 and starts with the words "Paraguayans, Republic or death we choose!" The composer's name is Francisco Acuña de Figueroa from Uruguay. He is also responsible for the Uruguayan national anthem. With so many countries gaining their independence and looking for songs to represent them, it must have been a booming business to write patriotic songs in those days!

RED, WHITE, AND BLUE

Paraguay enjoys the distinction of having an unusual flag. What makes the flag stand apart is that its two sides are different. Both sides have three horizontal stripes: red, white, and blue. In the center of the white stripe is a design. The design on the front is the national symbol—a yellow five-pointed star surrounded by a wreath of palm and olive branches tied with a red, white, and blue ribbon. Within the wreath are the words República de Paraguay (Republic of Paraguay) in black. The design on the back is the treasury seal—a yellow lion, a red cap of liberty, and the words Paz y Justicia (Peace and Justice) in blue.

The tricolor of red, white, and blue came to represent liberty, equality, and fraternity following the French Revolution that began in 1789. The French adopted these colors following the American Revolution. The two revolutions served as models for people seeking freedom all over the world, which is why you see so many flags using stripes in red, white, and blue. These colors originally came to America from the British flag called the Union Jack, which is also red, white, and blue.

INTERNET LINKS

http://www.nationalanthems.info/py.htm
This is a website containing the history and lyrics of Paraguay's national anthem.

http://www.visitparaguay.net/paraguay-guide/paraguay-festivals.html
This website contains information about a number of Paraguayan festivals.

FOOD

Here is an assortment of traditional Paraguayan foods.

PARAGUAYAN FOOD IS A BLEND OF Spanish-style cuisine and traditional Guaraní fare, with some Brazilian and other outside influences as well.

TRADITIONAL FOOD

Paraguayan food differs from that of Argentina, where meat predominates in the diet of even the rural poor. Meat is certainly important in the Paraguayan diet in regions where there is ranching, primarily the Chaco, but in the more populous eastern region, the standard diet derives more from the Guaraní heritage. In addition to manioc and corn, another commonly used ingredient is a homemade cheese made by local cheese makers.

Manioc and corn are usually used as flour. Corn is dried, then ground using a wooden mortar and pestle. Manioc can be reduced to flour in two ways: soaked for a week in water or mud, then dried in the sun and ground; or sliced, dried, and then ground.

Dishes made with corn flour include *mazamorra* (mah-zah-MOR-rah), a corn mush; *mbaipy so-o* (MBAY-pee SOH-oh), a hot corn pudding with chunks of meat; *bori-bori* (BOH-ree BOH-ree), chicken soup with corn flour balls; and *mbaipy he-e* (MBAY-pee AY-ay), a dessert of corn, milk, and molasses.

From manioc, there is *mbeyu* (MBEY-yoo), a manioc-flour pancake grilled much like the Mexican tortilla; and *chipa* (CHEE-pah), a manioc bread with eggs, cheese, fat, anise, and milk. There are many varieties of *chipa*, and it is eaten frequently during holidays, particularly Easter. Manioc can be eaten plain and boiled or roasted over coals. It is eaten as a side dish with almost every meal.

Stevia is a plant native to Paraguay. This leafy green plant, called "candyleaf" by the locals, has been used for centuries in traditional medicine as well as for a sweetener. Today, stevia has been adopted as a healthy sugar replacement due to its sweetness and lack of calories or carbs.

Soups are popular. *Soyo* (SOH-yoh) is a meat and vegetable soup, and *albóndigas* (ahl-BOHN-dee-gahs) is a meatball soup. Fish appears frequently at meals. The most popular are two freshwater species native to Paraguayan rivers: *surubí* and dorado. *Pira caldo* is a fish soup containing milk, cheese, onions, tomatoes, and sunflower oil. Beef and pork are the most popular meats. Paraguayan-style barbecue, or *asado*, is a common cooking method in which meat is cooked for a long period of time over a grill.

The national dish is *sopa Paraguaya*, or Paraguayan soup, which is not a soup at all but a cornbread that includes onions and cheese. *Chipa guazu* (CHEE-pah GWAH-zoo), a lighter variation, is a flat corn cake made with milk and fresh corn.

Special foods are too expensive for daily meals. *Sopa Paraguaya*, for example, is one that many people try to eat on Independence Day or during religious or family celebrations. Meat is also expensive, so barbecues are reserved for days like Christmas. On Christmas, families often make a picnic out of the barbecue to make the day extra special.

Essential rural kitchen equipment includes the mortar for pounding corn and manioc and a metal grater for grating manioc. Sieves for sifting flour are made from finely woven reeds. Many people put food in green bamboo sections to bake or boil on an open fire. Gas is more readily available in the cities, so people there cook using gas stoves.

BEVERAGES

Apart from soft drinks and tropical fruit juices, Paraguayans enjoy *mosto* (MOH-stoh), or chilled sugarcane juice. As you can imagine, this is quite sweet. Other favorite beverages are made from the yerba maté plant. As in Argentina and Uruguay, Paraguayans drink maté, a hot tea made from the leaves of this plant, which contain caffeine.

Carrulim, a Guaraní drink made of *caña*, *ruda* (a medicinal root), and lemon, is traditionally drunk on August 1. According to Guaraní beliefs, these ingredients drive away evil and keep a person happy and healthy. It is believed that those who do not drink *carrulim* on August 1 will have bad luck throughout the month of August.

The yerba maté plant was discovered by the Guaraní, who later taught the Spaniards how to drink maté tea. The scientific name for the plant, Ilex paraguayensis, *reflects the fact that Paraguayans popularized it. The Guaraní did not drink maté as a regular beverage; for them, it was a medicine. Maté contains a number of vitamins, including A, B1, C, and niacin, and has been demonstrated to be good for headaches and muscle aches. It is also a stimulant like coffee and increases the heart rate. Once the Spaniards discovered it, they made maté drinking a part of their lifestyle. From there, it came to represent a particular aspect of Paraguayan society.*

The traditional way to consume maté is from a special cup called a guampa *(gwahm-PAH), made from a cow's horn. The leaves are packed into the cup and hot water is poured over them. To drink the liquid without getting a mouthful of wet leaves, one uses a* bombilla *(bohm-BEEL-yah), or metal straw with mesh at the end, to keep out the leaves. Ideally, one does not drink maté alone, but in company. Each person drinks from the cup, then refills it with hot water and passes it to the next person. The whole time, of course, people are chatting and passing the time away. The favorite time to enjoy maté is during the cool mornings. People do not necessarily go through the ritual of passing the cup except on special or formal occasions, but they still enjoy sharing each other's company over a cup of maté throughout the day.*

DINING OUT

Eating out is very much an urban phenomenon. Few rural people can afford to eat out, and besides, they do not have access to restaurants. *Chipa* can be found at street food stalls across Paraguay. In major centers, there are many snack shops selling various breads and puddings along with the ever-present maté. Street vendors move around the city or board buses and trains to sell food to travelers. They provide everything from hot, cooked food to cool, refreshing beverages. This is the way people eat when traveling in Paraguay.

Loofahs are types of tropical and subtropical vines. Their fruit is grown to be harvested before maturity and eaten as a vegetable, popular in Asia and Africa. A loofah sponge is used like a body scrub, after the fruit is processed to remove everything but the network of xylem (ZAHY-luhm). However, this seemingly simple crop has greatly helped poor communities across Paraguay.

Thanks to the efforts of social activist Elsa Zaldívar in the early 2000s, the loofah has transformed impoverished areas throughout Paraguay. Zaldívar discovered that the loofah is an ideal cash crop and formed a collective of women to grow, harvest, and sell the plant. Paraguay's organically grown and harvested loofahs now boast an environmental and competitive advantage over many plantation-grown loofahs from China and other countries, and they provide a necessary source of income and opportunity for the people of Paraguay.

Not only has the loofah been able to bring in money for those who grow it, but the loofah is now helping to address Paraguay's housing problem as well. Working with industrial engineers, Elsa Zaldívar has combined readily available waste from the loofah with plastic waste to form strong, lightweight building panels. The panels are used to create furniture and construct houses, insulating occupants from temperature and noise. This innovation has addressed a real need in Paraguay, as many Paraguayan families lack adequate housing. When the panels break or fall apart, they can easily be broken down and recycled back into new panels, greatly easing the demand for wood in Paraguay's over-harvested forests.

Asunción boasts fancy restaurants. The typical formal restaurant is the *parillada*, specializing in grilled meat served with boiled manioc. Such establishments may offer their guests entertainment, usually a musical ensemble featuring the Paraguayan harp and guitar, and sometimes even *galopa*, or bottle dancers. Many Paraguayans never see the inside of a *parillada* restaurant because it is too expensive for them. For those who can afford it, a night out at a *parillada* is a social event.

In both Asunción and Ciudad del Este, there are quite a few Asian immigrants from Japan, China, and Korea. They have brought their cuisine with them, and now Paraguay is one of the best places in South America to find Asian food.

INTERNET LINKS

http://www.rolexawards.com/profiles/laureates/elsa_zaldvar
This website features information about Elsa Zaldívar's plastic creations and includes a video about the start and implementation of the project.

http://www.southamerica.cl/paraguay/typical-food.htm
This website describes traditional foods of Paraguay.

http://www.worldtravelguide.net/guides/south-america/paraguay/food-and-drink
This is a travel website with information about regional food and drink in Paraguay.

MBEYU

1 cup manioc flour
1 cup corn flour
Sprinkle of salt
6—8 tablespoons vegetable oil
½ cup (or less) milk or water
Crumbled cheese

Mix salt, manioc, and corn flour well. Add oil and mix by hand, crumbling flour chunks into tiny pieces. Gradually add milk, water, or a mix of the two and crumbled cheese to taste (cheese helps hold the batter together). Mixture should be somewhat dry.

Cover the bottom of an ungreased skillet with mixture ¼- to ½-inch thick, pressing it into the pan. Cook over medium heat until outside forms a light brown crust. Flip carefully and brown the other side.

Once cooked, remove from pan and enjoy plain or experiment with toppings.

CHIPA GUAZU WITH FRESH CORN

2 pounds fresh corn kernels chopped in a blender or food processor

Crumbled cheese for taste and texture

½ cup vegetable oil or butter

3 eggs, beaten

Salt to taste

Milk, enough to make the batter the consistency of thin cake batter

Chopped onions, to taste

Mix ingredients together, including cheese. Spread in greased 9-inch by 13-inch baking dish and bake at 350 degrees Fahrenheit until done in the center, between 30 and 50 minutes.

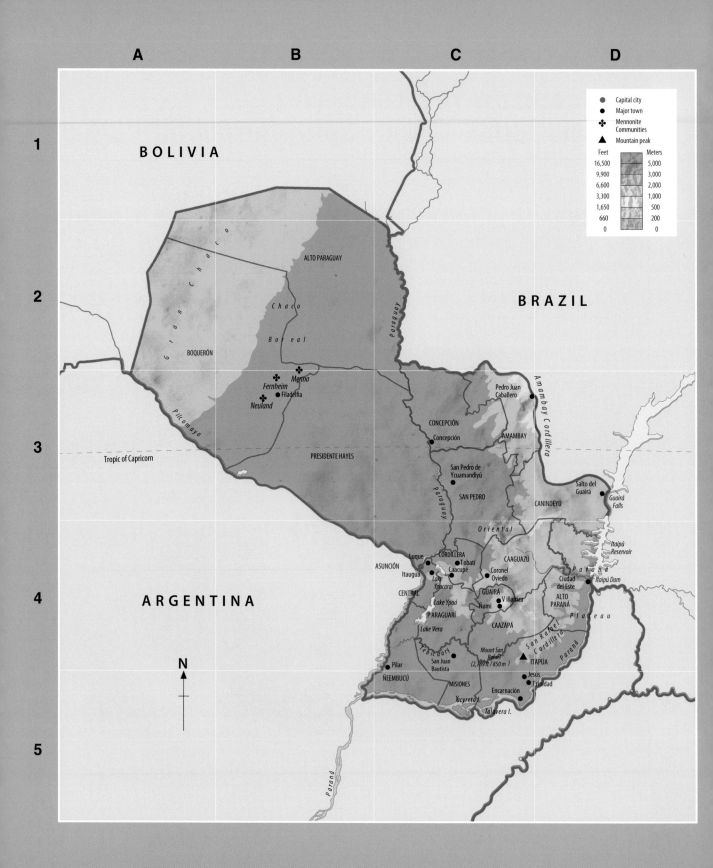

MAP OF PARAGUAY

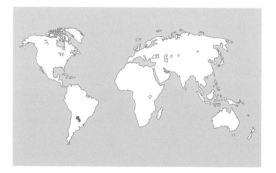

ECONOMIC PARAGUAY

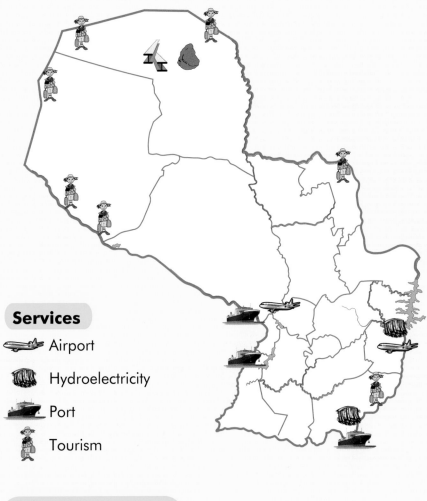

Services

✈ Airport

🔋 Hydroelectricity

🚢 Port

🧍 Tourism

Natural Resources

🪨 Iron ore

🪨 Maganese

ABOUT THE ECONOMY

OVERVIEW

Paraguay's economy is improving in the twenty-first century. It is marked by a large informal sector, which makes it hard to collect accurate economic data. This sector includes the re-export of imported consumer goods to surrounding countries, as well as numerous street vendors and other small, cash-based enterprises. Much of the population depends on agriculture to make a living. On average, incomes have grown over the last several years, as increasing world demand for commodities has combined with high prices and favorable weather to expand Paraguay's export trade.

GROSS DOMESTIC PRODUCT (GDP)

$29.62 billion (2017 estimate)

GDP GROWTH

4.3 percent (2017 estimate)

CURRENCY

Guaraní
$1 US = 5,628 guaranies (2017)

LAND USE

Arable land, 10.8 percent; permanent crops, 0.2 percent; permanent pasture, 42.8 percent; forest, 43.8 percent; other, 2.4 percent (2011 estimate)

NATURAL RESOURCES

Hydropower, timber, iron ore, manganese, limestone

AGRICULTURAL PRODUCTS

Cotton, sugarcane, soybeans, corn, wheat, tobacco, cassava (manioc, tapioca), fruits, vegetables, beef, pork, eggs, milk, timber

MAJOR EXPORTS

Soybeans, livestock feed, cotton, meat, edible oils, wood, leather, gold

MAJOR IMPORTS

Road vehicles, consumer goods, tobacco, petroleum products, electrical machinery, tractors, chemicals, vehicle parts

MAIN TRADE PARTNERS

Argentina, Brazil, United States, China, Chile, Russia

WORKFORCE

3.4 million (2017 estimate)

UNEMPLOYMENT RATE

6.5 percent (2017 estimate)

INFLATION

3.6 percent (2017 estimate)

EXTERNAL DEBT

$17.35 billion (2017 estimate)

CULTURAL PARAGUAY

National Park "Defensores del Chaco"
This national park covers an area of 1,780,900 acres (720,700 ha) and has a wide variety of vegetation and animal life. It also has the strong Cerro León, a unique geological formation in the Chaco, consisting of a succession of hills.

Cerro Corá National Park
This park protects an area of dry tropical forest and natural savanna within steep, isolated hills. It also has some interesting caves and petroglyphs. Rare birds, tortoises, armadillos, and monkeys can be spotted in the park.

Fernheim
This neat Mennonite community resembles a suburb of Munich planted in the middle of a red desert. Geometrically perfect homes line the streets in an orderly grid, with dusty roads and miles of Chaco wilderness extending beyond.

Itaipú Dam
The Itaipú Dam is the biggest dam in the world in terms of generating capacity. The dam is 643 feet (196 m) high, equivalent to a sixty-five-story building. The total length of the dam is 23,737 feet (7,235 m).

Asunción
Asunción is the home of the national government, principal port, and the chief industrial and cultural center of the country. The city is home to the Godoi Museum, the Church of La Encarnación, and the Metropolitan Cathedral.

Caacupé
Caacupé is the capital of the department of Cordillera. Caacupé is best known for *chipa* and the enormous basilica in the center of town to which thousands of Roman Catholics make their way each year on December 8 for the Feast of the Immaculate Conception.

Ciudad del Este
Ciudad del Este is the second-largest city in Paraguay. It is linked to the Brazilian city of Foz do Iguaçu by the Friendship Bridge, and also borders Argentina. It is most famous for its markets, both legal and illegal.

Ybycui National Park
Ybycui National Park preserves a remnant of what is known as the Brazilian rain forest in the low-lying hills of eastern Paraguay. It is a small park, but incredibly beautiful, consisting of undisturbed jungle and picturesque cascades.

Encarnación
Encarnación is home to a bustling shopping center, the heart of the Paraguayan Carnival, and the gateway to the nearby Jesuit ruins at Trinidad and Jesús de Tavarangue. The pleasant and functional modern town has excellent shops, a plaza, and modern facilities.

Trinidad Jesuit *Reducción*
The Jesuit *reducción* at Trinidad, just outside Encarnación, is a UNESCO World Heritage site. These historical ruins provide an amazing glimpse into the lives of the nearly four thousand indigenous people who lived here.

Ñacunday National Park
Ñacunday National Park is distinctive because of the Salto Ñacunday, the most important waterfall in the country. The park also has a wide variety of flora and fauna, and protects a stretch of the Ñacunday River, which is a habitat for a rich variety of fishes.

ABOUT THE CULTURE

OFFICIAL NAME
Republic of Paraguay

FLAG DESCRIPTION
Both sides have three horizontal stripes: red, white, and blue. In the center of the white stripe is a design. The design on the front is the national symbol—a yellow five-pointed star surrounded by a wreath of palm and olive branches tied with a red, white, and blue ribbon. Within the wreath are the words República de Paraguay (Republic of Paraguay) in black. The design on the back is the treasury seal—a yellow lion, a red cap of liberty, and the words Paz y Justicia (Peace and Justice) in blue.

TOTAL AREA
157,048 square miles (406,752 sq km)

CAPITAL
Asunción

ETHNIC GROUPS
Mestizo (mixed Spanish and indigenous) 95 percent, other 5 percent

RELIGION
Roman Catholic, 89.6 percent; Protestant, 6.2 percent; other Christian, 1.1 percent; other or unspecified, 1.9 percent; none, 1.1 percent (2002 estimate)

BIRTH RATE
16.6 births/1,000 Paraguayans (2017 estimate)

DEATH RATE
4.8 deaths/1,000 Paraguayans (2017 estimate)

AGE STRUCTURE
0—14 years, 24.56 percent; 15—64 years, 68.32 percent; 65 years and over, 7.12 percent (2017 estimates)

MAIN LANGUAGES
Spanish (official), Guaraní (official)

LITERACY
People age fifteen and above who can both read and write: 95.1 percent

LEADERS IN POLITICS
Alfredo Stroessner, 1954—1989
Andrés Rodríguez, 1989—1993
Juan Carlos Wasmosy, 1993—1998
Raúl Cubas Grau, 1998—1999
Luis Ángel González Macchi, 1999—2003
Nicanor Duarte, 2003—2008
Fernando Lugo, 2008—2012
Federico Franco (interim president), 2012—2013
Horacio Cartes, 2013—2018
Mario Abdo Benítez, 2018—present

TIMELINE

IN PARAGUAY	IN THE WORLD

3000 BCE
Guaraní widely scattered throughout central and southern America. Ancestor of thirty-seven Tupian language families settles in Paraguay.

116–117 CE
The Roman Empire reaches its greatest extent, under Emperor Trajan (98–117).

1206–1368
Genghis Khan unifies the Mongols and starts conquest of the world. At its height, the Mongol Empire under Kublai Khan stretches from China to Persia and parts of Europe and Russia.

1530
Beginning of transatlantic slave trade organized by the Portuguese in Africa.

1537 CE
Spanish begin colonizing the interior plains of Paraguay.

1776
Paraguay transferred from the Viceroyalty of Peru to the Viceroyalty of La Plata.

1789–1799
The French Revolution.

1808
Viceroyalty of La Plata becomes autonomous following the overthrow of the Spanish monarchy, but Paraguayans revolt against Buenos Aires.

1811
Paraguay becomes independent.

1864–1870
The War of the Triple Alliance.

1914–1918
World War I.

1932–1935
Paraguay wins territory in the west from Bolivia during Chaco War.

1939–1945
World War II.

1954
General Alfredo Stroessner seizes power, marks start of ruthless dictatorship.

1986
Nuclear power disaster at Chernobyl in Ukraine.

1989
Stroessner deposed in coup led by Andrés Rodríguez. Rodríguez becomes president.

1991
Breakup of the Soviet Union.

1992
New democratic constitution publicized.

1993
Juan Carlos Wasmosy wins first free presidential election.

1997
Hong Kong is returned to China.

IN PARAGUAY	IN THE WORLD
1998 Colorado Party candidate Raúl Cubas Grau elected president amid allegations of fraud.	
1999 President Cubas Grau resigns. Luis González Macchi appointed caretaker president, forms government of national unity.	
2000 Coup attempt foiled. Government blames "anti-democratic" forces loyal to exiled General Oviedo.	**2001** Terrorists crash planes in New York, Washington, DC, and Pennsylvania.
2003 Nicanor Duarte sworn in as president. Predecessor Luis González Macchi put on trial on corruption charges.	**2003** War in Iraq begins.
2004 Peasants stage series of land invasions and other protests, demanding redistribution of agricultural land.	**2004** Eleven Asian countries hit by giant tsunami, killing at least 225,000 people. **2005** Hurricane Katrina devastates the Gulf Coast of the United States.
2008 Leftist Fernando Lugo elected president, ending sixty-one years of conservative rule.	**2008** Barack Obama is elected president of the United States. **2009** Outbreak of flu virus H1N1 around the world.
2012 Fernando Lugo impeached following a violent land dispute.	
2013 Businessman Horacio Cartes elected president, putting the Colorado Party back in control.	**2016** Donald Trump becomes the US president. **2017** Two earthquakes in Mexico kill more than 350 people.
2018 Mario Abdo Benítez elected president.	

GLOSSARY

ahó poí (ah-HOH POY)
A very fine handwoven cotton cloth.

bombilla (bohm-BEEL-yah)
A straw used to drink maté.

capybara
A South American tailless rodent living along the banks of rivers and lakes, having partly webbed feet; the largest living rodent.

caudillos (cow-DEEL-yohs)
Political leaders who rule by threats and rewards.

cheolo (chay-OH-loh)
A man who comes out of the crowd to challenge the bull during the Festivals of Saint John and Saint Peter.

code-switching
Changing from one language to another, a speech characteristic of bilingual speakers.

encomienda (ayn-coh-mee-AYN-dah)
A system in colonial Latin America designed to give each Spanish colonists the right to hire cheap indigenous labor.

filigree
Delicate ornamental work of fine silver, gold, or other metal wires.

galopa (gah-LOH-pah)
Women's folk dance in which bottles are balanced on the head.

Jesuits
Catholic priests who belong to a group called the Society of Jesus. In Latin America, they were missionaries in the colonial period.

maté
Hot tea made from yerba maté leaves.

ñandutí (nyan-doo-TEE)
A cotton lace called "spider's web lace."

patron
Large landowner, boss of *peones*.

peon
Peasant indebted to a landowner or *patron*.

reducciones
Name given to Jesuit missions in South America.

shaman
An indigenous healer and priest.

syncretism
A blend of two or more sets of religious beliefs.

yerba maté
A plant and herb used to make maté, a kind of tea .

yopará (yo-pah-RAH)
An informal language that mixes Spanish and Guaraní terms.

FOR FURTHER INFORMATION

BOOKS

Salvatore, Mark. *Shade of the Paraiso: Two Years in Paraguay, South America: A Memoir.* Melbourne, Australia: Vine Leaves Press, 2018.

Stoesz, Edgar. *Like a Mustard Seed: Mennonites in Paraguay.* Scottsdale, PA: Herald Press, 2008.

Whigham, Thomas L. *The Road to Armageddon: Paraguay Versus the Triple Alliance, 1866—70.* Latin American & Caribbean Studies. Calgary, AB, Canada: University of Calgary Press, 2017.

WEBSITES

CIA World Factbook Paraguay. https://www.cia.gov/library/PUBLICATIONS/the-world-factbook/geos/pa.html.

Encyclopedia Britannica. https://www.britannica.com/place/Paraguay.

FILMS

Landfill Harmonic. The Film Collaborative, 2015.

Paraguay, 1945. National Archives and Records Administration, 2008.

Paraguay (PAL). TravelVideoStore.com. 2009.

MUSIC

The Great Paraguayan: Guitar Music of Barrios. Sony, 2005.

Los Diablos del Paraguay: Guaraní Music. Playasound, 2007.

Maiteí América: Harps of Paraguay. Smithsonian, 2009.

BIBLIOGRAPHY

Box, Ben. *South American Handbook*. Bath, UK: Footprint, 2011.

"Brazil to Triple Electricity Payments to Paraguay." BBC News, May 12, 2011. https://www.bbc.com/news/world-latin-america-13375638.

Buckman, Robert T. *Latin America*. The World Today Series. Lanham, MD: Stryker-Post Publications, 2011.

"Climate Paraguay." Climates to Travel. https://www.climatestotravel.com/climate/paraguay.

"Fernando Lugo." *Gale Biography in Context*, 2015. http://link.galegroup.com/apps/doc/K1618005027/BIC?u=buffalo_main&sid=BIC&xid=515aa048.

"In the Kitchen." *Somewhere in Paraguay*. https://somewhereinparaguay.com/paraguayan-recipes.

Itaipu Binacional. https://www.itaipu.gov.br/en.

"Mario Abdo Benítez." *Gale Biography in Context*, Gale, 2018. http://link.galegroup.com/apps/doc/K1650011039/BIC?u=buffalo_main&sid=BIC&xid=666c0d6d.

Mizen, Georgia. "6 Traditional Foods You Have to Try in Paraguay." *Culture Trip*, March 28, 2017. https://theculturetrip.com/south-america/paraguay/articles/6-traditional-foods-you-have-to-try-in-paraguay.

"Paraguay." UN Women. http://lac.unwomen.org/en/donde-estamos/paraguay.

"Paraguay Extends Zero Deforestation Law to 2018." World Wildlife Fund, September 3, 2013. http://wwf.panda.org/?210224/Paraguay-extends-Zero-Deforestation-Law-to-2018.

"Paraguay History." World Rover. http://www.worldrover.com/history/paraguay_history.html.

"Paraguay Passes New Law to End Violence Against Women, Including Femicide." UN Women, March 12, 2018. http://www.unwomen.org/en/news/stories/2018/3/news-paraguay-criminalizes-femicide.

"Paraguay Travel Guide." iExplore. https://www.iexplore.com/destinations/paraguay/travel-guides/central-and-south-america/paraguay/overview.

Sidder, Aaron. "Wildlife Dying En Masse as South American River Runs Dry." *National Geographic*, July 22, 2016. https://news.nationalgeographic.com/2016/07/pilcomayo-river-paraguay-caiman-capybara-fish-drought-death-water.

Tsioulcas, Anastasia. "From Trash to Triumph: The Recyled Orchestra." NPR, September 14, 2016. https://www.npr.org/sections/deceptivecadence/2016/09/14/493794763/from-trash-to-triumph-the-recycled-orchestra.

Turner, Blair. *Latin America*. The World Today Series 2017—2018. Lanham, MD: Rowman & Littlefield, 2017.

"The World Bank in Paraguay. World Bank. http://www.worldbank.org/en/country/paraguay.

INDEX

INDEX